Worlds of Shadow

Worlds of Shadow

Teaching with Shadow Puppetry

David Wisniewski and Donna Wisniewski

1997
TEACHER IDEAS PRESS
Libraries Unlimited
A Division of Greenwood Publishing Group, Inc.
Englewood, Colorado

TEACHER IDEAS PRESS
Libraries Unlimited
A Division of Greenwood Publishing Group, Inc.
P.O. Box 6633
Englewood, CO 80155-6633
1-800-237-6124
www.lu.com/tip

Project Editor: Judy Gay Matthews
Proofreader: Eileen Bartlett
Indexer: Linda Running Bentley
Interior Design and Layout: Judy Gay Matthews

Library of Congress Cataloging-in-Publication Data

Wisniewski, David.
  Worlds of shadow : teaching with shadow puppetry / David Wisniewski and Donna Wisniewski.
   xvii, 225 p. 22x28 cm.
   ISBN 1-56308-450-3
   1. Puppet theater in education. 2. Shadow puppets.
I. Wisniewski, Donna, 1947-   . II. Title.
PN1979.E4W57 1997
372.6'6--dc20   96-27720
                                          CIP

Table of Contents

Preface

The basic elements of shadow puppetry have been the same for almost 2,000 years: a light, a screen, and something to put between them to cast a shadow. When the art form began in India and China, the light was a flaming torch, the screen was a swath of cotton cloth, and the puppets were very elaborate figures of carved leather operated with long rods of animal horn. (See fig. Pref.1.)

Fig. Pref. 1.

None of this sounds very useful or practical for modern puppeteers, much less for teachers in today's classrooms. That's what we thought, too.

Then we hit a snag during the rehearsal of one of our first shows, *The Golden Candelabra*, a 1978 rod puppet production of a Persian folktale. The lights came up on an amply decorated stage. Gorgeous music and impressive narration began. And then . . . *nothing happened!* The narrator described jewel-like cities and crystal rivers and burning deserts, but all the audience saw was blue curtains. They were very nice blue curtains, but they couldn't take the place of seeing what the narrator was talking about.

We didn't want to bore the audience with a weak beginning. But we also didn't have the time or the money to craft cities, rivers, and deserts out of wood, Styrofoam, and papier-mâché. Then came a radical idea: Why not put a screen on the back of the puppet stage and *project* the scene on it from behind with an overhead projector?

After hastily stretching a white bedsheet over a wooden frame and bolting it to the stage, we located an old overhead projector and focused it on the screen. Then we cut the walls and towers of an ancient Persian city out of typing paper, added a wavy-edged piece of clear yellow plastic for the undulating desert dunes and a curved section of clear blue plastic for the river. We mounted the pieces on a transparency sheet with clear tape, put it on the projector, flipped the switch and . . . voila! The audience could now see everything the narrator was talking about. (See figs. Pref. 2 and Pref. 3.)

Fig. Pref. 2.

Fig. Pref. 3.

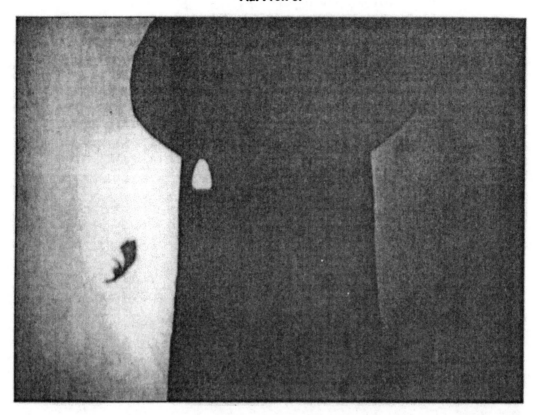

This new opening was greeted with enthusiastic "ooohs and ahhhs," so we decided to explore the medium further. We soon discovered that a lot of economical, everyday materials could create some pretty spectacular projected effects. Combining these techniques with inexpensive shadow puppets made of poster paper and a sturdier, more efficient plastic screen, we launched Clarion Shadow Theatre in 1980.

Besides offering performances to the region's schools, museums, and arts centers, we also conducted many shadow puppet workshops, sometimes as in-services for teachers and librarians, but more often for upper elementary school students. In these workshops, pupils spent ten to twelve hours of classtime creating shadow plays from scratch, receiving the initial story and role assignments on Monday and performing a finished production complete with music, sound effects, and narration on Friday. More than 5,000 children took part in these workshops, and each group put on a successful show. (See figs. Pref. 4 and Pref. 5.)

Fig. Pref. 4.

We also linked up with the Wolf Trap Institute for Early Learning Through the Arts. Sponsored by Wolf Trap Farm Park, the admirable performing arts park in Fairfax County, Virginia, the institute strives to integrate creative dramatics, movement, and music into the nation's Head Start curriculum. Our workshops with this organization over a ten-year period extended our range to younger children, prompting the development of many new visuals and exercises.

Fig. Pref. 5.

This book contains all the performance and workshop techniques we've developed over the past fifteen years, complete with shadow puppet patterns, scenery for transparencies, shadow screen directions, scripts, and rehearsal and performance hints. It is designed the same way we learned, in step-by-step fashion, progressing from the simplest figures and effects to multipart puppets and more complex visuals. We hope that those who work with children, whether they be teachers, librarians, camp counselors, scout leaders, or Sunday school teachers, enjoy the dynamic and dramatic new applications of this 2,000-year-old art.

Introduction

Shadow puppetry sounds rather exotic. Actually, it is, but only when you consider its ancient Chinese and Indian origins, its mystical ties to Eastern religions, and its present use in faraway lands such as Indonesia and Turkey. When modified and modernized, shadow puppetry becomes not only enormously practical but also the most vivid and flexible of puppet forms, not to mention the simplest and least expensive.

Here are some of the advantages we've discovered over the years:

1. *Less construction time:* All but the simplest hand puppets, rod puppets, and marionettes require sculpting, painting, and costuming. Three-dimensional scenery is equally time-consuming. Shadow puppets and projected scenery, however, are just drawn and cut out.

2. *Lower cost:* Other puppet forms demand the expense of paint, brushes, glue, papier-mâché, and sewing supplies. Shadow puppets require only paper, masking tape, and brass paper fasteners. Their operating rods are drinking straws or fondue sticks. Most of the materials used for projected scenery are inexpensive or are already in the supply room.

3. *Less mess:* Shadow theater is a completely dry construction process, eliminating the messy cleanup of wet art supplies.

4. *Fewer art skills required:* As mentioned earlier, shadow figures don't need to be sculpted or painted. Working in only two dimensions with a black shadow, you can make puppets as simple or as complicated as you wish. Also, many dramatic projected scenic effects are achieved with no art skill whatsoever. Besides, numerous puppet and scenery patterns are included, so you really can't go wrong.

5. *Less tiring and time-consuming rehearsal:* One of the great drawbacks of hand puppets, especially for children, is rehearsing with one arm up in the air. After five minutes, most student-operated hand puppets look like they've had heart attacks, crawling around the stage with their heads hanging off the edge. Rod puppets are a bit better in this regard, but shadow puppets are by far the easiest and most comfortable to manipulate. Also, because the projected image can be seen just as easily backstage as out in front, teachers can stay behind the screen to direct their students, a much more efficient rehearsal method than running back and forth.

6. *Greater range of visual effects:* We are still astounded by how many stunning visuals can be achieved with an overhead projector and an assortment of inexpensive materials. Pieces of wax paper turn into mountain ranges. Transparent colored plastic provides elegant sunrises

and sunsets. A strip of lace becomes a moving backdrop for a marathon runner. We discovered most of these effects right after we'd started our business and didn't have enough money for a movie. So we stayed home and put things on the overhead projector instead. If you find the simplicity of these images intriguing, you might do the same.

7. *Kids' familiarity with two-dimensional imagery:* Because of the inescapable influence of movies, television, and computers, even very young children now come to school with a savvy eye for 2D images. They are already used to seeing close-ups, scene changes, and shifts in perspective. Shadow theater capitalizes on this familiarity without furthering the passive behavior associated with it.

The last point was completely missed by a teacher who once reproached us after a performance. "I hope you realize how much your shadow theater looks like television," she sniffed.

"I hope you realize how much television looks like our shadow theater," Donna replied. There may be a superficial resemblance, but all similarities end with the screen. Rather than passive viewing, shadow theater provides active individual and group participation in the writing, planning, construction, rehearsal, and performance of a live production.

After the basics of light and screen are taken care of in Chapters 1 and 2, the book divides into shadow puppetry for younger children (ages 3–7) and shadow puppetry for older children (ages 8–12). The latter builds on the former, however. Many of the most captivating visuals are in the chapters for younger children, whereas some of the more complex effects in the later chapters are not beyond the reach of primary grades. So feel free to explore as far as you and your students wish. Plug in the overhead projector and let's get started!

Light

Unless an angry mob is attacking the school in search of the PTA treasurer, the use of flaming torches as a light source is usually not a good idea. So we'll proceed to evaluate more acceptable lighting instruments.

LIGHTING INSTRUMENT CHOICES

1. *Desk lamps:* Although these little lights are inexpensive and often have spring clips or clamps to attach them to the shadow screen or backstage tabletop, they give limited and unfocused light. (See fig. 1.1.) No projected image is possible with them, so all puppets and scenery have to be up on the screen. However, when fitted with a ten-watt bulb and a cardboard or blue acetate shade, they're great for low-level backstage safety lighting.

Fig. 1.1.

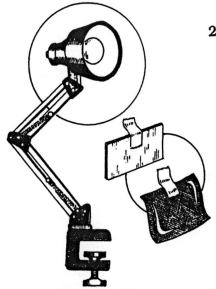

2. *Bulbs with reflectors:* Almost all hardware stores carry circular reflectors to which you can add hundred-watt clear bulbs and spring clips for quick and inexpensive lighting. (See fig. 1.2.) Again, however, the light is limited and unfocused with no possibility of projection.

Fig. 1.2.

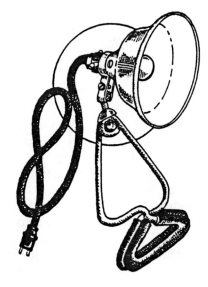

3. *Opaque projectors:* These bulky machines project images from books and papers with clarity and brightness, but changing scenes is awkward and visually jarring. (See fig. 1.3.)

Fig. 1.3.

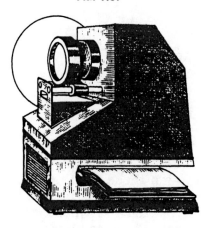

4. *Slide projectors:* A terrific variety of bright, crisp imagery is possible with these instruments, but all subjects have to be photographed and turned into slides, a lengthy and moderately expensive process. (See fig. 1.4.) Scene changes are clumsy because the screen goes dark when slides shift. Although a dual fade control or the use of two slide projectors would lessen the problem, why not just use an overhead projector?

Fig. 1.4.

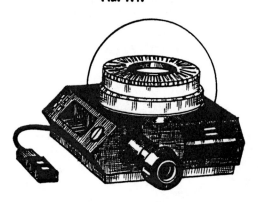

5. *Overhead projectors:* Now we're talking! These machines project with the brightness and clarity of slide projectors but offer much more flexibility. (See fig. 1.5.) Their large projection stages, usually a 10" to 12" square, allow all scenes to be on inexpensive compact transparencies, which are a breeze to change. Equally important, the instrument's magnifying properties yield a tremendous amount of visual variety. Not only do everyday materials assume totally new visual properties, but giant characters and big scenic effects can be achieved with much more ease and believability on the overhead projector than against the shadow screen. Although these machines aren't cheap (a basic machine costs around

$250 new), they're very common. Almost all schools have one or two stashed away in the audiovisual (AV) room, as do many corporations and some churches. Used overhead projectors are sometimes available from AV supply stores. Any overhead projector can be used for shadow puppetry. Some models may offer brighter light, a wider angle of projection, bulb changers, or a closed lens head instead of the open flip-up kind. Newer portables even include the bulb in the same housing as the lens, with light reflecting off the projection stage instead of going through it. But even if yours has three missing legs and a switch made of petrified chewing gum, don't worry. It'll work fine for now.

Fig. 1.5.

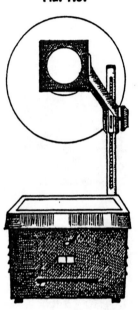

FRONT PROJECTION VERSUS REAR PROJECTION

Overhead projectors are most often used in front of a movie screen or blank wall. Although this front projection is ideal for classwork, it works against dramatic performance because the audience sees the puppeteers. (See the upper section of fig. 1.6, page 4.) Also, the entire production then has to be performed on the projection stage of the overhead projector, severely limiting the size of puppets, the variety of scenic effects, and the number of performers.

Putting the overhead projector behind the screen solves all these problems. As the lower section of figure 1.6 shows, the shadow screen conceals the performers so that they are no longer a distraction to the audience. Unbound from the projection stage of the overhead projector, the production can now utilize larger puppets, full scenic effects, and more puppeteers against the shadow screen.

Rear projection does require a translucent shadow screen, however. Regular movie screens are opaque and won't transmit light and shadow. But don't worry! The directions for making simple shadow screens are coming right up in Chapter 2.

Fig. 1.6.

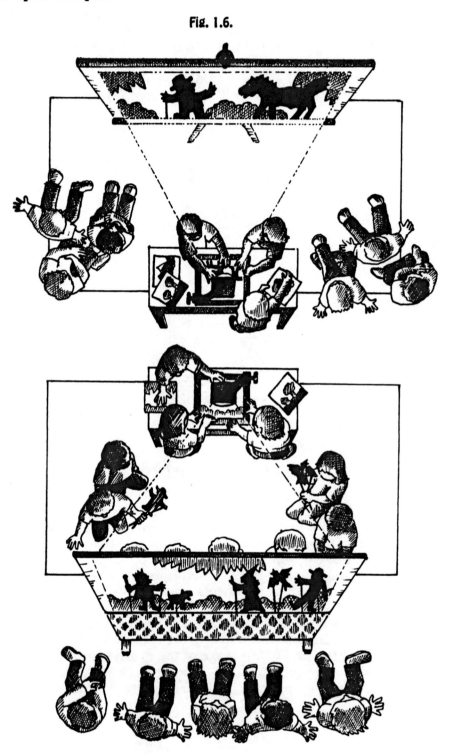

Screen

The shadow screens in this chapter range from the very simplest tabletop variety to full-length freestanding versions capable of staging *Gone with the Wind*. First, we'll talk about some common screen materials, then about how to frame them.

SCREEN MATERIAL CHOICES

1. *Paper:* Although wide rolls of white art paper are inexpensive and readily available, they result in screens that are fragile and impossible to clean.

2. *Sheet:* A white sheet is sturdier than paper, but its weave lets through a lot of light, creating an uncomfortable "hot spot" that shines directly into the audience's eyes. This poor light diffusion also causes a drastic falloff in image quality when viewed from an angle.

3. *Plastic shower curtain liner:* Costing just a few dollars, a plain white shower curtain liner is rugged enough for classroom use and offers better light diffusion than a sheet.

4. *RoscoScreen Twin-White:* This excellent product is made expressly for image projection and is by far the best screen material. A tough and cleanable plastic with terrific light diffusion properties, RoscoScreen Twin-White costs about $15 a yard. With a 55" width, even one yard makes a fair-sized screen. (When attaching it to the frame, please note that the matte surface of the material faces the audience while the glossy side stays backstage.) Because the Rosco company manufactures the material for large-scale theater use, it's easier to order the yard or two necessary for a shadow screen through a theatrical supply store. If there isn't one in your area, contact our friendly neighborhood supplier: Kinetic Artistry, 7216 Carroll Avenue, Takoma Park, MD 20912 (Tel: 301-270-6666, Fax: 301-270-6662). Service representatives will be more than happy to answer any questions about the product and ship your order within a week.

FRAMING CHOICES

1. *Old picture frame:* If a sturdy wooden picture frame with exterior measurements of at least 36" x 48" is residing in your basement or attic, fasten the screen material to the back with ¼" heavy-duty staples to create an adequate shadow screen. It will be necessary to attach a piece of 1"-x-2" lumber to the back of the picture frame so that it can be anchored to a tabletop with a 3" C-clamp. (See fig. 2.1.)

Fig. 2.1.

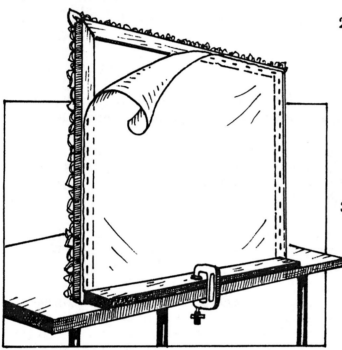

2. *PVC pipe:* Lengths of 1¼"- or 1½"-diameter PVC pipe can be connected with PVC right angles to form a rectangle. (See fig. 2.2.) The screen can be attached with self-stick Velcro patches instead of staples. Because round stock does not clamp securely to a flat table, add a piece of 1"-x-2" lumber to the base for secure operation.

3. *Stretcher strips:* Available at art and craft supply stores, these interlocking wood pieces provide the framing for an artist's canvas. (See fig. 2.3.) They come in standard sizes of 8" to 60" in 2" increments and can also be special-ordered in longer lengths and thicker stock. After gluing the stretcher strip joints and fitting them together to form a frame, staple the screen material in place with ¼" staples. If more portability is required, assemble the joints without glue and attach the screen material with self-stick Velcro patches.

Stretcher strips are wide enough for the frame to be C-clamped to the table without any additional support. The audience will see the stapled side of the screen, but that's of no concern once the lights go down and the show begins. However, if you prefer, hide the staples by adding a 1"-x-2" clamping strip to the back of the frame after the screen material has been attached.

Fig. 2.2.

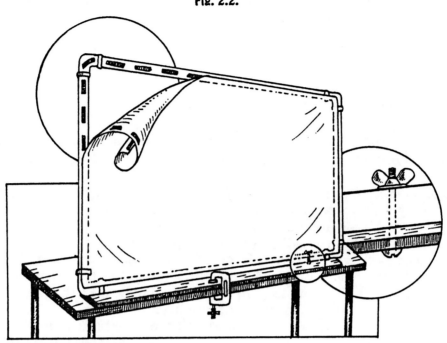

Fig. 2.3.

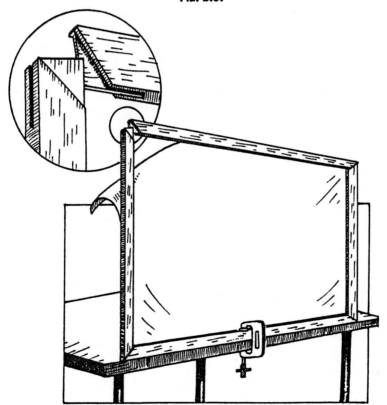

4. *1"-x-2" lumber:* Basic carpentry skills will be necessary for constructing a wooden frame from scratch.

TABLETOP SHADOW SCREEN

■*Supplies:* saber saw or circular saw, two 36" lengths of 1"-x-2" lumber, two 48" lengths of 1"-x-2" lumber, eight 6" right triangles of ¼" plywood, wood glue, ¾" nails, hammer, combination square, staplegun with ¼" staples, a 3" C-clamp, miter box, and saw (miter box and saw are optional)

■*Directions:* Cut lumber and plywood to size with saber saw or circular saw. If using a miter box and saw, cut 45-degree angles on both ends of the four pieces of 1"-x-2" lumber. If not, butt the pieces together with the 36" pieces to the outside of the 48" pieces. (See fig. 2.4.)

Glue one end of a 36" piece and a 48" piece, as well as the back of one plywood triangle. Fit the joint together and square it with the combination square. Then align and nail the plywood triangle over the joint with ¾" nails. Do this to all four joints and let them dry.

Turn the frame over. Glue and nail the remaining four plywood triangles over the joints. When dry, staple the screen material to one 48" length; then stretch it moderately and staple it to the other side. Staple the other two sides, keeping the screen material tight, but not so tight that it knocks the frame out of plumb.

Trim away any excess screen material and clamp the completed shadow screen to the edge of a table with the 3" C-clamp.

Fig. 2.4.

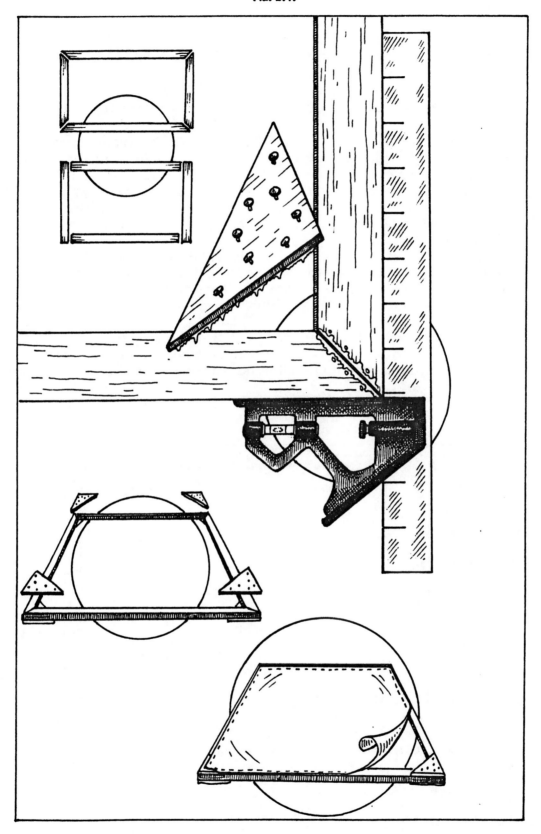

FOLDING TABLETOP SHADOW SCREEN

The frames made of stretcher strips or 1"-x-2" lumber can be made to fold in half, allowing larger screens and easier storage.

■*Supplies:* saber saw or circular saw, combination square, two 3" strap hinges with screws, drill with bit smaller than screw width, screwdriver

■*Directions:* Before attaching the screen, mark the exact center of the top and bottom of the frame with the combination square. Cut the frame in half with a saber saw or circular saw.

Keeping the frame together, place a 3" strap hinge over each cut and mark where the screws go. To stop the wood from splitting, drill a hole smaller than the width of the screw at each mark. Then screw the strap hinges in place. (See fig. 2.5.)

Attach the screen material, but remember that it must be stapled to the same side of the frame as the hinges so that it folds within the frame when shut. (Because of the 1"-x-2" clamping strip on the back of the picture frame and the roundness of PVC pipe, hinges won't work on frames made of these materials.)

For classroom workshops, we use a 42"-x-66" shadow screen that folds to a compact 42"-x-33" size. This size accommodates a fair number of students backstage without requiring a lot of distance between the overhead projector and the screen.

Fig. 2.5.

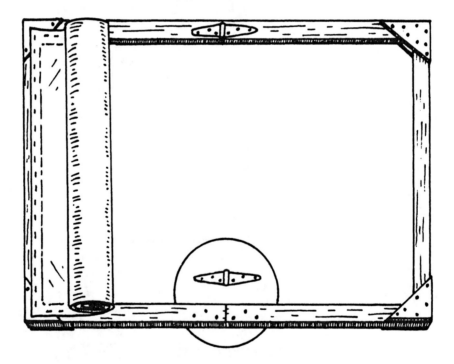

LARGER TABLETOP SHADOW SCREEN

It's possible to enlarge the screen to take advantage of the RoscoScreen Twin-White's full width of 55 inches. We can expand the 42"-x-66" proportions of our classroom workshop screen, for instance, to reach exterior measurements of 55" x 86" (folding to 55" x 43"), approximately the size we use for theater performances. (See fig. 2.6.)

Remember, though, that the overhead projector will require more room backstage to light the screen. This might make a larger screen too awkward for classroom use, but it will work well in a multipurpose room or gymnasium for bigger audiences.

Fig. 2.6.

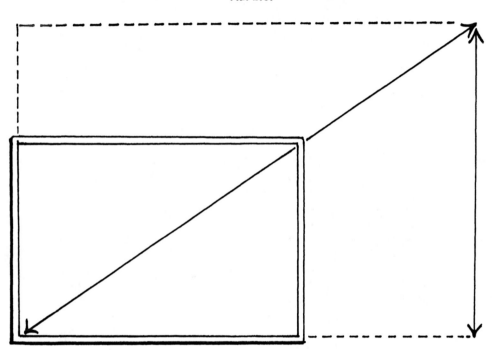

In the classroom, a tabletop screen doesn't really require masking for informal presentations. But if students are going to perform before their peers or parents in a larger room, it's worthwhile to skirt the table and use side curtains if possible. (See fig. 2.7.) Because the students have to kneel behind a tabletop screen, backstage gym mats or carpet squares help prolong rehearsal time and ensure a more comfortable performance.

Fig. 2.7.

FREESTANDING SHADOW SCREEN

With the addition of side supports, the screen can be raised so that students can stand for the entire performance.

■*Supplies:* saber saw or circular saw, two 96" pieces of 2"-x-2" lumber, four 36" pieces of 1"-x-4" lumber, electric drill and ¼" drill bit, four 4"-long ¼" machine bolts, four 5"-long ¼" machine bolts, eight ¼" wing nuts, eight ¼" flat washers, and eight ¼" lock washers

■*Directions:* Center and square two 36" pieces of 1"-x-4" lumber on either side of each 96" piece of 2"-x-2" lumber. (See fig. 2.8, page 14.) Clamp and drill two holes through all three pieces of wood with ¼" drill bit. Fasten with 5"-long ¼" machine bolts, flat and lock washers, and wing nuts.

Clamp shadow screen to side supports with bottom of frame at average forehead height of your students. Drill two holes on each side through both pieces of wood with ¼" drill bit and fasten with 4"-long ¼" machine bolts, flat and lock washers, and wing nuts.

Stand shadow screen upright. Anchor bottom of each support with a couple of fabric-padded bricks or 5-pound exercise weights. Warn children to walk around supports rather than stepping over them. Screen open area below shadow screen by stapling fabric in place.

Fig. 2.8.

FULL-LENGTH FREESTANDING SHADOW SCREEN

We have occasionally used RoscoScreen in a double width of 110 inches for very large presentations. This extra width is helpful if you want to use full-length human shadows against the shadow screen in conjunction with shadow puppets on the overhead projector. However, shadow puppets operated against the full-length screen won't work because puppeteer shadows will also be seen. (See fig. 2.9.)

In any case, the widths of RoscoScreen need to be held together. An inexpensive 2"-wide transparent tape is available from Rosco for temporarily joining the material. The RoscoScreen should be butted together rather than overlapped, as a double thickness will cause a dark line across the shadow screen. Apply the tape to the backstage glossy side of the material only. (Rosco also offers two widths welded together permanently, but that runs the price up to $90 a yard. So unless a distant relative left a bequest, stick with the tape for double-width screens.)

When you construct such a large screen, increase the lumber size to 1"-x-4" and construct more substantial side supports.

These 2"-x-2" poles are the most basic side supports. The following section on larger freestanding shadow screens includes directions for sturdier framed supports of 1"-x-4" lumber. They can be used singly (see fig. 2.10, page 16) or in sets of two (fig. 2.11, page 17) to support this smaller freestanding shadow screen.

Fig. 2.9.

Fig. 2.10.

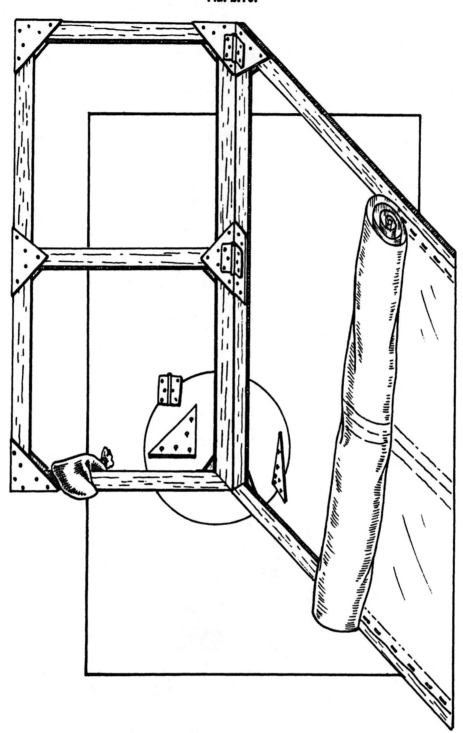

Fig. 2.11.

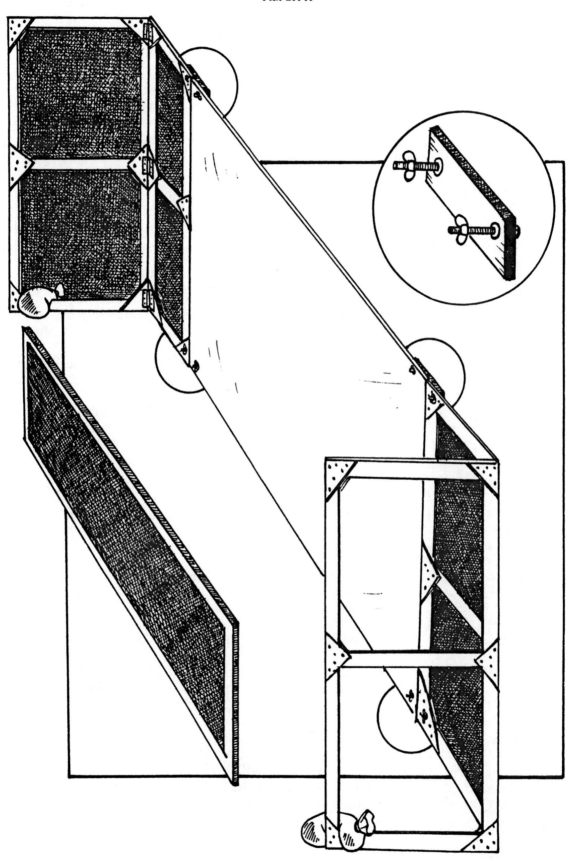

■*Supplies for Full-Length Shadow Screen:* saber saw or circular saw, two 96" pieces of 1"-x-4" lumber, two 144" pieces of 1"-x-4" lumber, eight 10" right triangles of ¼" plywood, ¾" nails, hammer, wood glue, combination square, staplegun with ¼" staples, two 6" strap hinges (optional)

■*Directions for Full-Length Shadow Screen:* Construct shadow screen frame of 1"-x-4" lumber and reinforce corners with 10" right triangles of ¼" plywood. (See directions and figure 2.4 for tabletop shadow screen.) Add strap hinges if 12' length of screen will cause storage problems. (See directions and figure 2.5 for folding tabletop shadow screen.) Do not attach screen material yet.

■*Supplies for Side Supports:* saber saw or circular saw, four 96" pieces of 1"-x-4" lumber, six 30" pieces of 1"-x-4" lumber, twenty-four 10" right triangles of ¼" plywood , two 3½"-x-10" rectangles of ¼" plywood, six 4" loose-pin hinges, wood glue, ¾" nails, hammer, screwdriver, combination square

■*Directions for Side Supports:* Cut 1"-x-4" lumber for side supports to size and lay out per figure 2.10. Glue one corner joint and square with combination square. Glue and nail reinforcing triangle in place. Repeat for all corner joints.

Glue ends of middle 1"-x-4" piece and center it. Glue and nail triangles in place. Let dry; then turn side supports over and add additional triangles to corners and middle 1" x 4"s.

Lay side supports down flanking shadow screen frame and attach trio of 4" loose-pin hinges to tops of reinforcing triangles. (Glue and nail 3"-x-10" rectangles of ¼" plywood to sides of shadow screen frame to accommodate middle hinge. Make sure the pinheads are uppermost when you attach the hinges!)

Attach screen material; then fold side supports in and raise shadow screen. When upright, unfold side supports and weight each with 10-pound sandbag or exercise weight.

Like the 2"-x-2" supports, these side supports are attached to the edges of the shadow screen. Student actors will have to be careful not to bump into them when entering and exiting. (The projected shadows, of course, won't have any problems at all!) The side supports can swing a little bit beyond the recommended right angle to provide more room without unbalancing the screen. But if additional space is desired, consider building "books" of side supports: two supports hinged together flanking the shadow screen. (See fig. 2.11.)

Follow the previous directions for side supports and figure 2.10, doubling the lumber supplies to make four side supports. After hinging the supports into "books," attach them to the full-length shadow screen with 8" sections of 1"-x-4" lumber bolted with 4"-long ¼" machine bolts, washers, and wing nuts.

Heavy fabric attached to the side support facing the audience will hide the actors. However, side curtains will still be necessary to prevent the audience from seeing backstage. Covering both side supports of a "book" will allow the shadow screen to be used without side curtains.

If you want to use shadow puppets against this full-length screen, a piece of heavy cloth can be stretched across the length of the screen. To prevent the cloth from drooping, attach the top to a length of 1"-x-4" lumber or frame the piece completely. A couple of 2"-long ¼" machine bolts with washers and wing nuts will hold the masking in place. Either solution will provide the "floor" for shadow puppets to walk on in addition to hiding puppeteer shadows.

PLACING THE OVERHEAD PROJECTOR

Now it's time to place the overhead projector behind the screen. There is no mathematical formula as to how far back the overhead projector has to be. It depends on the width of the screen and whether the instrument has a wide-angle lens. Machines with a wide-angle lens produce a wider field of light than a standard lens, allowing the overhead projector to be closer to the screen. (See fig. 2.12.)

Fig. 2.12.

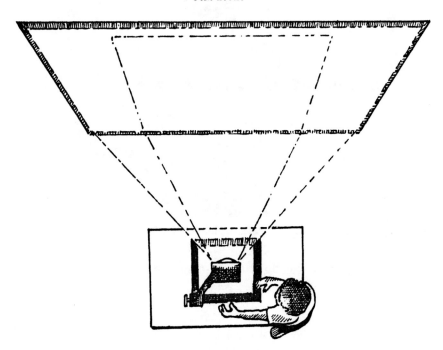

Line up the lower edge of the projected light with the bottom of the screen; then focus the light so that it fills the screen from side to side. Because the overhead projector emits a square of light, there will be light projected above the rectangular shadow screen. This "spill" can be prevented by taping a piece of paper across the upper part of the glass projection stage of the projector. You'll see the projected edge of the paper on the screen, so just line up the shadow with the top of the shadow screen. (See fig 2.13, page 20.)

Fig. 2.13.

Great! Now that the light and screen are taken care of, we'll move on to what goes between them.

3

Introducing Shadows
(Ages Three to Five)

If you are working with very young children aged three to five, it is best to introduce the concept of shadows to them before vaulting directly into shadow puppets. The following activities were developed in Head Start classrooms during our association with the Wolf Trap Institute for Early Learning Through the Arts. The italicized text is suggested narrative to accompany the exercises. Feel free to use examples and expression comfortable to you and your classroom environment.

ACTIVITY 1: MEETING YOUR SHADOW

Supplies: overhead projector, shadow screen

Directions: After setting up the overhead projector and focusing the light on the shadow screen, turn off the machine and seat the children in front of the screen. (Make sure that it's clamped to a low table so that the children will cast shadows from at least the chest up—see fig. 3.1.)

Fig. 3.1.

"When it's a sunny day outside on the playground, what do you see on the ground underneath you? That's right! A shadow. Do you have a shadow on a very cloudy day? Do you have a shadow on a very dark night? No, you don't. You must have light to have a shadow.

"Look up at the lights on our ceiling. When they're on, does your hand have a shadow? Hold your hand close over the floor and let's see . . . yes, it does. Now, I'll turn the lights off. Ooops! The shadow from your hand is gone. You must have light to have a shadow.

"Now, I'll turn on the overhead projector behind this white screen. Is the light from the projector brighter than the ceiling lights? I think so, too. Do you think we can cast shadows with this light? Let's find out!"

Place one hand directly behind the shadow screen to cast a shadow. (See fig. 3.1.)

"What do you see? That's right! You see the shadow of my hand. You can't see my hand because it's behind the white screen, but you can see the shadow of my hand. Now what do you see?"

Place your head directly behind the shadow screen in profile and continue talking.

"That's right! You see the shadow of my head. Can you see my lips move when I talk to you? I thought so. My shadow moves when I move. Now, I'm going to wave at you."

Raise one hand above the shadow screen and wave at your students. Keep waving as you lower it behind the shadow screen.

"See? My shadow moves when I move! Let's take turns behind the shadow screen to see if everyone's shadow moves when they move."

Invite the children backstage to cast their shadows, individually or in small groups. Ask them not to look into the overhead projector's light but to face their shadows on the shadow screen. Have them move to demonstrate that their shadows do whatever their bodies do.

"Thank you for coming backstage so nicely and remembering not to look into the projector's light.

"Now, reach up to the sky. Very good! Now, jump up and down! Well done. Wave at everyone in the audience. Good! I think everyone's shadow is moving when they move."

ACTIVITY 2: FINDING YOUR PROFILE

■*Supplies:* overhead projector, shadow screen

■*Directions*: With the children seated in front of the shadow screen, kneel behind it and face forward so that the shadow of your head is cast on the screen.

> *"Can you see the shadow of my head? Good. What parts of my head can you see in shadow? Hair . . . ears . . . gee, that's about all. But wait . . ."*

Turn your head to the side to show your profile.

> *"Now what can you see? Hair again . . . but also nose, eyelashes, mouth, teeth, even my tongue. You see much more of my face when I turn to the side. When you see my face from the side like this, it's called my profile.*
> *"Who wants to show off their profile?"*

Have students come up one at a time and ask the class how they know whose profile is on the screen. (See fig. 3.2.) As all facial features become apparent in profile, be careful how students feel about things like glasses or protruding teeth. Most children of this age simply accept these things as part of their distinctive profile, but a few are sensitive and dislike any attention brought to them.

Fig. 3.2.

"How do we know for sure this is Clarissa's profile? Yes, she has a ponytail. Are you sure that this is Mark's profile? That's right! Mark is wearing glasses.

"Mark, would you take your glasses off for a moment? Can you still tell this is Mark's profile? Yes, Mark's nose turns up at the end, just like his Daddy's."

ACTIVITY 3: GUESSING PROFILES

■*Supplies:* overhead projector, shadow screen

■*Directions:* Seat the children in front of the shadow screen; then have them close their eyes and ask them not to peek.

"I'm going to tap one of you on the head. That person can come up to show their profile on the shadow screen. Then I'll ask everybody to open their eyes and look at the profile. Raise your hand if you know who it is and I will call on you. Nobody peek now! Promise?"

ACTIVITY 4: OPACITY

■*Supplies:* overhead projector, shadow screen, three pieces of construction paper (one black, one red, and one yellow)

■*Directions:* Hold the black construction paper above the shadow screen. In a moment, lower the paper so that it casts a shadow. (Unless your room can be darkened considerably, please don't press the papers against the screen because ambient light from windows and skylights can cause lighter colors to show up through the screen. Hold the colored papers an inch away from the screen to retain a black shadow, as shown in figure 3.3.)

"Who can tell me what color shadow this black paper will cast? Very well, let's see. Yes, you're right. The black paper casts a black shadow.

"Now, who knows what color shadow this red paper will cast?"

Hold up the red construction paper and bring it down behind the screen.

"The red paper casts a black shadow, too! Was anybody surprised by that?

"Well, then, let's try the yellow paper. What color shadow will it cast? How about that? The yellow paper also casts a black shadow. Does anybody know why?"

Hold all of the pieces of paper behind the screen.

"The paper stops light, just like our bodies stop light. So it casts black shadows just like our bodies, even though the paper is much, much thinner. When something stops light, it is opaque. Because the paper is opaque, does it matter what color it is for casting shadows? No, not even a little bit!"

Hold the papers in front of your eyes a moment.

"Can you see through something that is opaque? No, not at all."

Fig. 3.3.

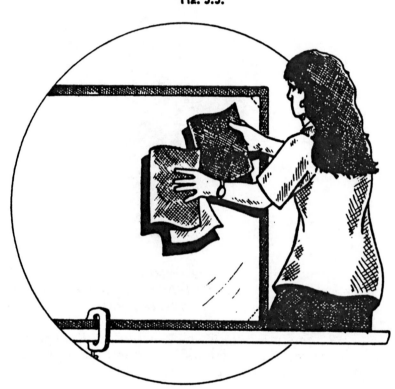

ACTIVITY 5: TRANSPARENCY

■*Supplies:* overhead projector, shadow screen, one clear transparency, two pieces of differently colored clear plastic (red and yellow, for instance)

■*Directions:* If not already in the supply room, transparent sheets of colored plastic are often available at office supply stores. The colored cellophane used for gift wrapping is also usable. Or when you order the RoscoScreen Twin-White, ask for a free swatchbook of Roscolux, which is used to color stage lights. The swatches aren't very big, but they're fine for this exercise.

Begin by holding the clear transparency above the shadow screen. Be ready to lower it. (See fig. 3.4, page 26.)

Fig. 3.4.

"*There are some things that don't stop light at all. This clear plastic is one of them. Look around the room for a moment. Is there anything else that doesn't stop light at all? That's right . . . the glass window! And Mark's glasses, too!*

"*When something is so clear that all the light goes through, it is transparent. This plastic is transparent. Do you think it will cast a black shadow? No! You can barely tell it's there.*"

Hold the pieces of clear colored plastic above the screen, one in each hand. Again, lower them in a moment.

"*These pieces of plastic are also transparent, but one is red and the other is yellow. Do you think that these will cast black shadows? No shadows at all, but see how well the red and yellow colors show up? Transparent things show their colors very nicely against the white screen.*"

Look through the transparency and colored plastic at the children.

"*Can you see through something that is transparent? Yes, indeed! I can see you and you can see me.*"

ACTIVITY 6: TRANSLUCENCE

■*Supplies:* overhead projector, shadow screen, wax paper

■*Directions:* Hold a sheet of wax paper above the screen and be ready to lower it.

> *"Other things let a little bit of light through. They don't stop light like paper, so they're not opaque. They don't let all the light through like clear plastic and glass windows, so they're not transparent. These things are sort of in between. They are called translucent.*
> *"This wax paper is translucent. Let's see what it looks like behind the screen. Instead of a black shadow, it makes a gray shadow. Some light gets through, but not a lot. It's translucent."*

Hold the wax paper in front of your eyes. (See fig. 3.5.)

> *"I can see through the wax paper a little bit. Can you see me? A little bit? Can you see me clearly? No, it's hard to see through something that's translucent."*

Fig. 3.5.

ACTIVITY 7: MAKING SHADOWS GROW

■*Supplies:* overhead projector, shadow screen

■*Directions:* Besides introducing the magnifying qualities of the overhead projector, this activity is effective for reinforcing the concepts of big and little, bigger and smaller, and growing and shrinking.

Turn on the overhead projector and place your hand directly behind the screen.

> *"Do you remember how I put my hand behind the screen to cast a shadow? Good! This shadow is exactly the same size as my hand. But there's a way I can make this shadow much bigger. Watch . . ."*

Keeping your hand's shadow cast on the screen, step back to the overhead projector. The shadow will become bigger, but also gray and indistinct. Then place your hand on the glass projection stage. Its shadow will be magnified and in focus. (See fig. 3.6.)

"Wow! Now it's huge! I put my hand on the overhead projector. It made the shadow of my hand much bigger. Now, I'll make the shadow smaller again."

Fig. 3.6.

Move your hand from the glass projection stage to the front of the lens and step back to the shadow screen. The shadow of your hand returns to normal size. This sequence can be repeated by you or by individual students.

"All right, Andrea has her hand behind the screen. The shadow is getting big, bigger . . . biggest! It's biggest when Andrea's hand is on the projector. Now, move back to the screen, Andrea. The shadow is getting small, smaller . . . smallest!"

Vary this activity by using such things as pencils, paper clips, scissors, and string.

Sometimes, an enlarged object becomes mysterious enough to warrant a guessing game. For instance, place a ring on the overhead projector; then turn it on. Stand next to the screen and thread your hand through the ring's projected shadow. (See fig. 3.7.)

"Look! Somebody left their bracelet on the projector. I wonder who it belongs to. Gosh, it fits so nicely. Maybe I'll keep it. What? It's a ring? Really? Boy, I can't fool you guys at all!"

A pair of glasses can be very funny on the overhead projector. After placing them, go behind the screen and center your head between the lenses. (See fig. 3.7.)

Sometimes, children ask for shadows of living creatures such as fish, flies, crickets, and earthworms on the overhead projector. Needless to say, this is a bad idea. However, there's no reason you can't make a cutout of a creature.

Fig. 3.7.

ACTIVITY 8: RIDING A SHADOW HORSE

■*Supplies:* overhead projector, shadow screen, cutout horse

■*Directions:* This exercise not only uses a shadow puppet for the first time but also acquaints you with image reversal. If you place your hand on one side of the projection stage, for instance, you'll see that the shadow is projected on the opposite side of the screen. (See fig. 3.6.) This happens with front projection as well as rear projection. It takes a bit of getting used to, especially when coordinating movements on the projector and the screen. (Which is what we're going to do right now. Yow!)

Reproduce the accompanying horse (fig. 3.8) on a copy machine, enlarging it if you wish. Transfer the pattern to any medium color of construction paper or poster paper with carbon paper, cut it out, and place it against the screen. After finding the shadow too small to ride, move the cutout to the overhead projector. (Remember, image reversal will cause the shadow to face the opposite way from the puppet on the projector.) Center the shadow on the screen.

> *"Is this shadow horse too small to ride? How can we make it bigger? That's right! We'll put the horse on the overhead projector. There! Now the horse is big enough to ride.*
> *"Christopher, would you like to ride this shadow horse?"*

Move the horse backward to make room for the student's shadow. Lower the horse's head to be within reach of the student's hand. (See fig. 3.9, page 32.) When interacting with student shadows, keep shadow puppet movements on the overhead projector small and slow. The actions are greatly magnified on the screen, and deliberate, subtle movements allow students to keep up.

Fig. 3.8.

From *Worlds of Shadow.* © 1996. Teacher Ideas Press. (800) 237-6124.

Fig. 3.9.

"Christopher, would you like to name the shadow horse? Sunshine? That's a great name. Would you like to pat her on the forehead? She likes that.

"You know, Sunshine might be hungry. Would you feed her? That's right, just hold your hand out flat.

"Why don't we go for a ride on Sunshine?"

Lower and center the shadow so that the student can hold the horse's mane.

"Sunshine is ready! Hop on top. Now hold tight to the mane. Get ready to move along with Sunshine, Christopher."

Move the horse forward off the projection stage, taking care to keep student and horse shadows together as much as possible. After a bit of practice, students might enjoy a longer ride. After leaving the projection stage, turn the horse around and bring it back. Move the horse slowly so that students can place their bodies and hands.

This activity can be varied by using different animals. On the following pages are patterns for an elephant, a whale, and a dinosaur. (See figs. 3.10, 3.11, page 34, and 3.12, page 35.) Like the horse, they can be copied and enlarged before transferring them to other paper and cutting them out.

(Text continues on page 36.)

Fig. 3.10.

Fig. 3.11.

Fig. 3.12.

ACTIVITY 9: TRANSPORTATION ("The Wheels on the Bus")

■*Supplies:* overhead projector, shadow screen, cutout bus

■*Directions:* The procedure for this exercise is identical to the previous activity except that the subject changes to transportation and centers on the song "The Wheels on the Bus." After cutting out the bus (fig. 3.13), show it to the students by placing it against the screen. Then bring it to the overhead projector and slowly enter it from the side of the projection stage. Stop when the driver's window and steering wheel come into view. (See fig. 3.14, page 38.)

> *"This bus is certainly too small to ride in. Yes, you're right. We'll put the bus on the overhead projector. Here it comes! I think we need some engine noise . . . vrooom! That's better."*

Appoint a bus driver and introduce the song.

> *"Karen, would you like to drive the bus? Great! Come behind the screen and hold on to the steering wheel of the bus. Now, when I move the bus, that steering wheel is going to move. So you hold on and move with it, all right? The song starts like this:*

> The wheels on the bus go
> Round and round,
> Round and round,
> Round and round.
> The wheels on the bus go
> Round and round
> All through the town.

> *"Now, we'll all sing together. Karen, start up your bus. Vrooom! Off we go . . ."*

As in the previous exercise with Sunshine, turn the bus around and slowly enter it from the side of the projection stage it just left. Repeat the verse if necessary. Make sure your driver is still in the driver's seat. Get ready to stop.

> *"All right, Karen. The bus is coming back. Here comes the steering wheel. Hold on to it and drive the other way. Vrooom! Now, put on the brakes. Squeeeak! We've stopped. Hey, you're a good driver! Now, we need passengers on the bus."*

Additional verses fit the characters on the bus. For instance, we often use a mother and father with a crying baby. One parent holds the baby while the other tries to quiet it.

Move the bus forward on the projection stage so that a couple of windows can be seen. The mother and father board the bus and place themselves in the window openings. (See fig. 3.14, page 38.) When the bus starts, it gently bounces in place rather than exiting.

Fig. 3.13.

Fig. 3.14.

"*Austin, would you be the daddy holding the baby? Thank you. Elizabeth, would you be the mommy? Thank you. All right, climb on board the bus. Stay in the windows so we can see you. Karen, start the bus. Vrooom! Here we go . . .*"

The baby on the bus goes,
"Waa, waa, waa,
Waa, waa, waa,
Waa, waa, waa."
The baby on the bus goes,
"Waa, waa, waa."
All through the town.

The mommy on the bus goes,
"Keep that baby quiet.
Keep that baby quiet.
Keep that baby quiet."
The mommy on the bus goes,
"Keep that baby quiet."
All through the town.

The daddy on the bus goes,
"Shh, shh, shh,
Shh, shh, shh,
Shh, shh, shh."
The daddy on the bus goes,
"Shh, shh, shh."
All through the town.

These verses can be repeated with other students taking the parts of the parents, or new passengers with new verses can come on board. To make room for new passengers, previous riders can get off the bus or the driver can ask them to "move on back" in one verse. New passengers can pay for the ride with a verse saying, "The money on the bus goes, 'Chinga-linga-ling.' " Other verses can comment on the ride: "The ride on the bus is bumpy and rough" and "The people on the bus go up and down."

To end the activity, slowly move the bus forward off the projection stage. Again, try not to lose your driver or any passengers.

This exercise can also be varied by using different modes of transportation. The following pages have patterns for a train, a ship, and an airplane. (See figs. 3.15, page 40, 3.16, page 41, and 3.17, page 42.) Remember to adjust the final stanza of the verse for some of these vehicles. A train might chug "all through the town," but a ship would be better off sailing "all across the sea"; and an airplane is more believable if it flies "all through the sky."

Fig. 3.15.

Fig. 3.16.

Fig. 3.17.

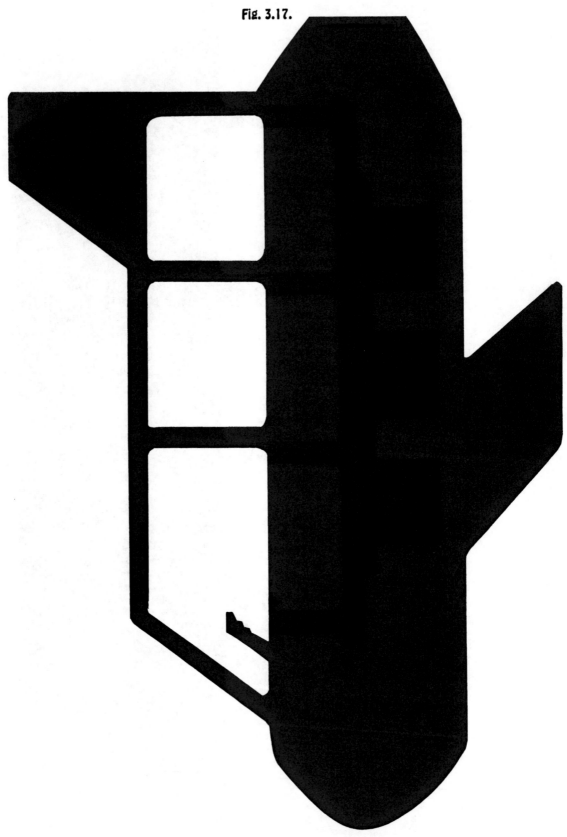

4

Simple Shadow Puppets
(Ages Three to Seven)

Now that the youngest children have been introduced to the concept of shadows and the basic use of the overhead projector and shadow screen, it's time to extend the age range a little bit and make some actual shadow puppets for student use.

Because of the age spread, the shadow puppet patterns in this chapter range from simple cutouts for ages three to five to uncomplicated figures with one moving part for ages six to seven. (The moving part is drawn as an option so that the same pattern can be used for both age levels. Circles indicate holes for the paper fasteners that attach moving parts. Control rod locations are marked with an X.)

For upper age level students who'd like to design their own shadow puppets but feel a little shaky in the sketching department, we've included a section about using basic shapes to draw.

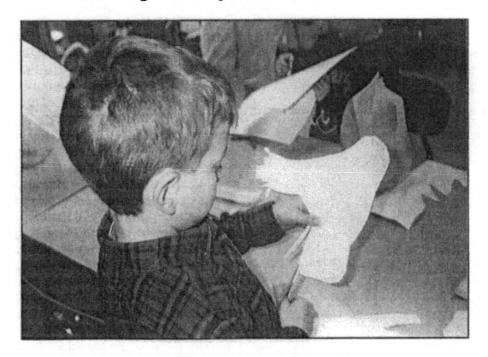

SHADOW PUPPET CUTOUTS FOR AGES THREE TO FIVE

Because of the children's elementary cutting skills, it's often best for teachers and aides to cut out the shadow puppets for this age level. Doing this outside of class usually saves time and energy. As with previous patterns, reproduce them on a copier, enlarging them if you wish.

1. *Paper:* Construction paper is fine for shadow puppets without moving parts. It's easy to cut and figures can be easily repaired with masking tape. If you'd like the puppets to be more durable, use a lightweight poster paper.

   In either case, use a medium color (rather than dark blue or black) so that cutting lines show up better. As mentioned in Chapter 3's opacity activity (see fig. 3.4), white or light-colored paper might show up through the shadow screen if your room has a lot of ambient light. If this happens even with medium colors, darkening the room or holding the puppets an inch away from the screen will result in better shadows.

2. *Control rods:* Use masking tape to stick the upper part of a flex straw to one side of the shadow puppet. (See fig. 4.1.) The straw should be located toward the top of the figure so that it doesn't flop backward over the straw. For additional length, crimp the end of a regular straw, insert it into the end of the flex straw, and tape it in place. (Don't use another flex straw for extra length, because the additional bend will make the figure almost impossible to operate.)

   If a student has difficulty gripping the straw, tape a toilet paper tube to the straw for a more comfortable handle. Should the straw prove too flimsy, use a thin dowel rod with the tape tab described in the control rod section for ages 6–7.

Fig. 4.1.

3. *Decoration:* This step is optional but sometimes strangely necessary. If you showed students the concept of opacity in Chapter 3 (Activity 4), they know that shadow puppets will cast black shadows. However, that doesn't stop the majority from wanting to color them in anyway. If decoration seems inevitable, don't put control rods on the cutouts yet because they'll only get in the way of enthusiastic artists.

   Crayon and marker won't show up in shadow, of course, but other things will. Eyes made with a hole punch can be covered with clear colored plastic. (See fig. 4.2.) The same holds true with decorative spots and stripes. (Just don't make so many that the puppet falls apart!) Use clear tape to stick the plastic to the puppet. (Frosted tape blocks light almost as much as masking tape.) Pieces of clear colored plastic can also be used for hair and clothing. Feathers and yarn are possibilities, too.

Fig. 4.2.

4. *Operation behind the shadow screen:* After control rods have been attached, the first thing most children do with a shadow puppet is whirl it around like a flag. The second thing they usually do is whirl it around another shadow puppet, causing both to tear. Although this damage is repairable, it's better to prevent it in the first place. So a few rules are helpful.

"*Rule number 1: Take care of your shadow puppet. When not using it on the shadow screen, please keep it flat on the table or cradled in your hands. Please don't operate your shadow puppet in midair. The paper might rip, and the tape on the control rods gets loose. Please don't leave your shadow puppet on the floor because crunch!—somebody could step on it. And please don't use any shadow puppet other than your own. That could start an argument, and that would mean I put all the shadow puppets away for today.*"

"*Rule number 2: Kneel behind the tabletop shadow screen. Kneeling keeps your body small, and you can move quickly out of the way when your turn is over. Can you move quickly when you're sitting on your bottom? No way! Keep your bottom down on your feet. That keeps your head from popping up on the shadow screen.*
"*Let's all try kneeling like that one time.*"

Kneel on the floor to the side of the shadow screen. (See fig. 4.3.)

Fig. 4.3.

Now move behind the shadow screen and press the shadow puppet against it. Be prepared to hear about how much your head shows!

> *"Rule number 3: Press your shadow puppet against the screen. Pardon me, Juan? My head shows? Well, that's because I'm taller than you guys. As I was saying, press the shadow puppet against the screen. That keeps it nice and flat for a good shadow.*
>
> *"Now, let's take turns putting our beautiful shadow puppets on the screen. Form a line to the side of the shadow screen and go through one at a time. When you finish, go back to your place and sit down."*

This last rule can be enhanced with a few helpful hints:

Helpful Hint 1: To turn a shadow puppet around, lift it back from the screen a tiny bit and twist the control rod. Then press the shadow puppet back against the screen.

Helpful Hint 2: Don't move the shadow puppets too fast. If shadows of eagles, tigers, race cars, and rocket ships zip by too quickly, the audience won't know what they were. Besides, all those decorations need to be seen and appreciated.

Helpful Hint 3: Try to enter and exit the shadow puppets from the sides of the shadow screen. Unless a character lives underground, it's more believable to see figures moving on and off the screen like actors on a stage.

Helpful Hint 4: Because this is a new experience for everybody, have students take turns moving their shadow puppets across the screen in one direction only, usually from stage left to stage right. (These directions refer to an onstage actor's left and right and are illustrated further in figure 6.15, page 125.) This stops bodies as well as shadow puppets from getting tangled up.

If the children eventually perform a story, rhyme, or song that requires their puppets to meet and move in opposite directions, some backstage traffic control might be necessary. Hints about that are in this chapter's next section for ages six and seven.

5. *Operation on the overhead projector.* After trying their shadow puppets on the screen, the students will certainly want to see their creations magnified by the overhead projector. This requires moving the shadow puppet on the projection stage while watching the giant result on the shadow screen. Some of the children may not have developed the ability to split focus enough to accomplish this easily, so please take this step slowly and on an individual basis. (See fig. 4.4, page 48.)

Fig. 4.4.

As before, a few ground rules help:

> *"Rule number 1: Please don't look directly into the overhead projector's light. It's very bright. Have you ever had your picture taken with a flash bulb? Did you see spots afterward? Well, that can happen if you look into this light. You might trip and fall if you see spots instead of where you're walking. So please don't look into the light."*

Most children of this age level stick their shadow puppets on the projection stage in haphazard fashion. Rather than explain the confusing issue of image reversal, keep it simple by pointing out that the bottom of the projection stage is aligned with the bottom of the shadow screen. (See fig. 4.5.)

Fig. 4.5.

"Rule number 2: Luisa, would you please come up to the shadow screen and show us the bottom part of the screen? Thank you. Keep your finger there one moment. I'll go back to the overhead projector and show the bottom part of the glass stage where you put the shadow puppets.

"Can everyone see the big shadow of my finger near Luisa's finger? Good. The bottom part of the projector's glass stage shines right where the bottom part of the shadow screen is. If you make your shadow puppets walk along the bottom part of the projector's glass stage, the giant shadow will walk along the bottom of the shadow screen.

"Let's take turns making giant shadows walk back and forth. I'll be back here to help you. Please form a line to the side of the shadow screen. Come up to the overhead projector one at a time. When you finish, please go back to your seat."

SHADOW PUPPETS WITH ONE MOVING PART FOR AGES SIX TO SEVEN

Most older students should be able to handle the cutting of these simple shadow puppets. Those that do need a helping hand sometimes profit from learning how to cut an inside corner without turning scissors around. (See fig. 4.6.)

Fig. 4.6.

1. *Paper:* The choice of paper really depends on how long you want the shadow puppets to last. For a one-time project, construction paper is fine, but for repeated use, lightweight poster paper is preferable. It also stands up better to the wear and tear of moving joints. Again, using a medium color ensures better cutting line visibility.

2. *Assembly:* The single moving part of these shadow puppets requires only minimal assembly. (See fig. 4.7.) Cut the moving part as an entirely separate piece from the main body of the puppet. (Don't cut the moving part out of the main body. If you do, you won't be able to put the puppet together!)

Overlap the moving part with the main body of the puppet. Use a pencil as a pivot point and move the part around. If you like the placement, punch a hole through both pieces of paper with a hole punch. Insert and spread a ¼" or ½" brass paper fastener. (See fig. 4.7.) Longer brass paper fasteners will work, but they sometimes stick out beyond the edge of the puppet. If they do, just bend the fasteners back over themselves one time.

Fig. 4.7.

3. *Control rods:* Beginning with this age level, we sometimes use 12" bamboo food skewers for control rods. I say "sometimes" because the sticks are pointed at one end. Although this end gets covered with masking tape and stuck to the shadow puppet, we always let the teacher decide whether to use them. Besides being inexpensive and available at most grocery stores, bamboo food skewers are thinner and stronger than straws.

Because these sticks do not have the built-in bend of a flex straw, a bend needs to be made of masking tape. (Clear and frosted tapes don't hold on to wood very well.) Just take a few inches of 1"-wide masking tape and adhere it lengthwise past the pointed end of the food skewer. (See fig. 4.8.) Then wrap the tape around the stick. This makes a bendable tape tab at the end of the control rod. Tape the tab to the upper part of the shadow puppet as close to the end of the stick as possible. Otherwise, the little bit of tab between the end of the stick and the shadow puppet bends so much that control becomes difficult.

Fig. 4.8.

These tape tabs give shadow puppets and their moving parts much more range and flexibility. Let's say a shadow puppet ship has to capsize and sink. If the control rod is simply stuck to the back of the ship, your hand will show when you turn the ship over. (See fig. 4.9.) The tape tab bends when you twist the control rod, allowing you to upend the ship with your hand still out of sight.

Fig. 4.9.

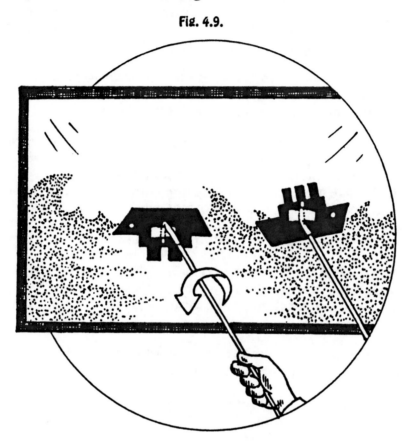

Unlike with the solid cutouts in the previous section, it sometimes matters which side of these shadow puppets you put the control rods on. To be on the safe side, put both control rods on the same side as the moving part. (See fig. 4.8.) If the control rods are on the other side, the rod for the moving part can bump into the main body of the puppet and restrict movement. Please don't put a control rod on each side, as that stops the puppet from being properly pressed against the screen.

For extra length, overlap another stick by at least two inches and completely wrap the joint with masking tape. As noted earlier, a toilet paper tube can be taped to the control rod for better direction by students with grip problems.

4. *Decoration*: If only a few students whip out their crayons after their introduction to opacity, you might consider nipping this unseen adornment in the bud. You can then proceed to decorations that actually show (as described earlier) or skip these frills altogether.

5. *Operation behind the shadow screen*: The first set of rules about shadow puppet care, proper kneeling, and pressing the shadow puppet to the screen are still necessary. Because these puppets have moving parts, though, the third rule needs a slight addition:

> "*Rule number 3A: Press the main control rod of your shadow puppet firmly against the shadow screen to stop it from wobbling around when you operate the moving part.*"

The helpful hints about turning shadow puppets around, controlling quick movements, making proper entrances and exits, and keeping backstage movement uncomplicated are still essential as well.

Backstage movement will get more complex as the students move beyond beginning exercises into the informal performance of short songs, rhymes, and stories. (Chapter 6 includes a number of techniques to simplify it.) For right now, though, all you need are hints for traffic control:

Traffic Control Hint number 1: An alternative to lining up students for individual screen crossings is to give a group of four or five students a couple of minutes to try out their shadow puppets. This option needs to be followed immediately by . . .

Traffic Control Hint number 2: All shadow puppets must stay on the screen first. The overhead projector can be used later.

Traffic Control Hint number 3: If shadow puppets must collide, participants must agree that one puppet stays pressed against the screen while the other operates a few inches away from the screen. That way, shadows, rather than puppets, crash into each other. (See fig. 4.10.)

We often demonstrate this with our hands before the students try out their puppets. Stand to the side of the shadow screen and thump your fists together behind it. Students see and hear the collision of fists and shadows. Then separate your fists and make the same movement. Voila!—shadow contact without physical impact!

6. *Operation on the overhead projector*: Most of these older children should be more comfortable dividing their attention between the shadow puppet on the overhead projector and the magnified shadow on the screen. If so, it's worthwhile to explain image reversal. (See figs. 3.6 and 3.9.) Be careful not to get entangled in different viewpoints of left and right.

Fig. 4.10.

"Sean, may I borrow your shadow puppet for a moment? Thank you. Before you try your shadow puppet on the overhead projector, take a look at this. When I enter the shadow puppet from the right side of the glass stage, the shadow gets projected on the left side of the screen. If I enter it from the left side of the glass stage, the shadow ends up on the right side of the screen.

"The shadow of your puppet will move in the opposite direction to the way you move it on the projector. I really don't know why this happens, but at least now we won't be surprised by it."

Pointing out the alignment of the bottom of the projection stage with the bottom of the shadow screen is appropriate at this point (see fig. 4.5); so is the caution about not looking directly into the projector's light. (One second-grader took this warning very seriously. We noticed him working very industriously, so we turned our attention to other students. He came backstage with not only a shadow puppet but a pair of poster paper sunglasses with red plastic lenses.)

If the class is not too tired or overstimulated by these activities, let them play with their creations against the screen and on the overhead projector. A lot of worthwhile interactions take place as the students acclimate themselves to the medium.

DRAWING WITH BASIC SHAPES FOR AGES SIX TO SEVEN

Although it's certainly efficient to use shadow puppet patterns, it's usually deemed more creative to draw them from scratch. But that's not always practical. Besides time constraints, there's also the issue of disproportionate drawing skills. Some children have natural talent in this area. Others don't. And some of them would rather jump off a bridge than draw.

And what about the teacher? If your drawing skills are weak, how can you help those who are lagging behind or hopelessly baffled? The following may not solve the problem completely, but we've found it to be a great help.

Donna was trained as a graphic designer rather than a fine artist. Working with pictures and type was easy, but translating her ideas into drawings was a frustrating chore. What was in her head would just not come out her pencil. She found that working with basic shapes enabled both her and her students to get their ideas across.

> *"How many people in this class like to draw? That's great. And how many people in this class feel kind of so-so about drawing? Well, I certainly understand. When I was your age, I felt exactly the same way. In fact, I felt the same way even when I grew up.*
>
> *"But, you know what? I found a way to draw that's not so hard. You use basic shapes. I'm sure you already know them."*

Go to the blackboard and, with the class identifying the shapes as you go along, draw a circle, an oval, a square, a rectangle, and a triangle. (See fig. 4.11.)

Fig. 4.11.

The development of the first drawn subject is charted in figure 4.12 and parallels the following narrative:

> *"With these shapes, you can draw just about anything. Let's start off with some animals. How about a pig? Which one of these shapes is a pig's body shaped like? That's right! A big, fat oval.*
>
> *"The pig's head is what shape? Correct! It's a circle. But where does it go? Above his body or more out in front? Yes, it's out in front . . .*
>
> *"And what about the front of the pig's head? His snout? It's kind of a square . . .*
>
> *"You connect the head to the body with a neck shaped like a . . . rectangle!*
>
> *"His ears? Triangles. How many? Two.*
>
> *"And his legs are . . . rectangles. Long, skinny ones? Or fat, stumpy ones? Yes, I think fat and stumpy would look good, too.*
>
> *"But what about his tail? Is that like any of these shapes? No, we'll have to fudge that one a little bit. There, it looks like a triangle that somebody sat on.*
>
> *"Now, let's look at our pig. Can it be mistaken for any other animal? No way. That's definitely a pig. What next?"*

Fig. 4.12.

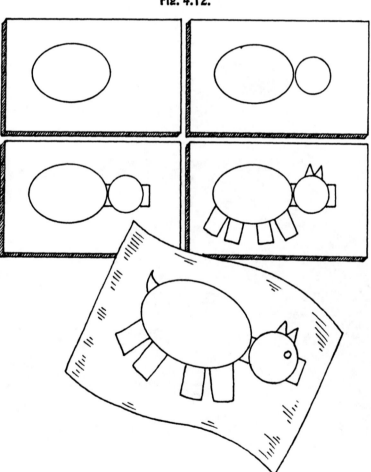

The following pages contain a number of animals and characters made with basic shapes. They're each drawn sequentially from the first shape through the completed basic figure. (See figs. 4.13, 4.14, page 60, and 4.15, page 61.)

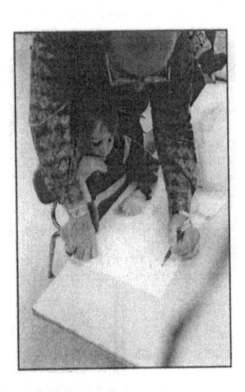

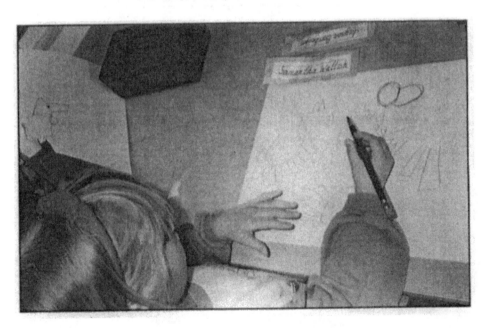

(Text continues on page 62.)

Fig. 4.13.

Fig. 4.14.

Fig. 4.15.

Because these shadow puppets are being drawn from scratch, they require a few ground rules that their patterned compatriots have no need of. The first rule is actually for teachers and is best illustrated by figure 4.16.

The silhouette on the left is the shadow of the pig drawn with basic shapes. The silhouette on the right is the shadow of the same thing drawn by a first-grader terrified of drawing. He was ecstatic with his creation.

Fig. 4.16.

"Rule number 1: Basic is basic."

Some of the shadow puppets may strain adult conceptions of what something should look like, but they are many children's prodigious first efforts at trying to visualize and express things for themselves. All of their attempts are valid, and considering what some children overcome, many are masterpieces.

The more accomplished young artists in your class may have to be reminded of this:

Raoul: *Teacher! Teacher! Patty's horse looks like a mutant caterpillar!"*
Teacher: *"Stop it, Raoul."*

Now, on to the other ground rules, all displayed in figure 4.17.

"Rule number 2: Please make your shadow puppet big enough to be seen. If you draw something really tiny, people are going to look at it up on the screen and say, 'What is that? Is that a germ or something?' So make your shadow puppet at least ten inches tall. The bigger you draw it, the easier it will be to cut out. It'll be easier to make a moving part and put control rods on it, too.

"Rule number 3: Make sure that all the heads, tails, arms, and legs of your puppet are good and wide where they attach to the body. For instance, what if your puppet has a skinny neck. What could happen? That's right. His head could fall off!

Fig. 4.17.

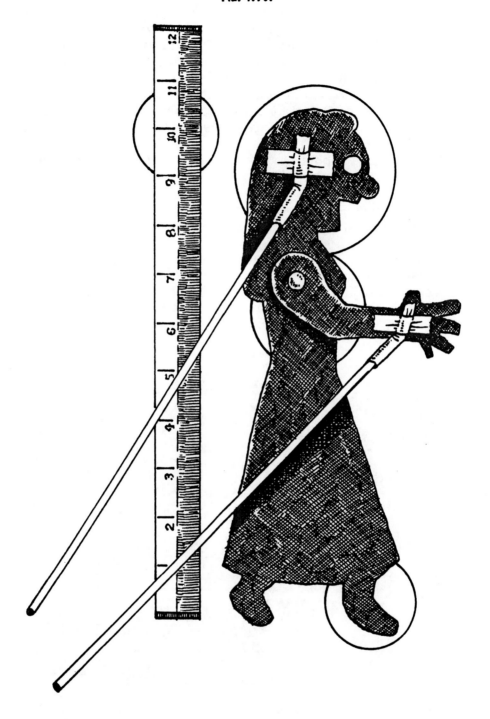

"Rule number 4: Now that we're talking about heads, I have a question. Do you think it's better to draw your characters with their heads facing you or from the side? That's right. Draw them from the side. Draw them in . . . profile! That's the word I was looking for. Do you remember when we first talked about profiles? (See Chapter 3, Activity 2.)

"You can do so much more with profiles. You can cut around the head instead of sticking your scissors in the paper to cut out the eyes, nose, and mouth. Your puppets can turn around. They can face other characters.

"Can shadow puppets do that if they're looking forward all the time. No way!"

These four rules are enough if the students make only cutouts. But if shadow puppets with moving parts are wanted, the process needs to be explained.

First, go to the blackboard and draw the handsome fellow in figure 4.18. The transformation of this figure from cutout to shadow puppet with moving part is charted to parallel the narrative. (If a hands-on demonstration is better for your students, the same narrative can be used with the cutout in figure 4.19.)

Fig. 4.18.

Fig. 4.19.

Please note that the overlap of the moving part is rounded. Though not important for this fellow's shoulder joint, it becomes very important for elbows, knees, and waists. Straight cuts are exposed when bent; rounded cuts blend into each other.

"Let's say that this fellow is a shadow puppet. Does he have any moving parts? No, he's just a cutout. But what if I want his arm to move? What is the first thing I'm going to have to do to that arm? It's going to sound terrible. That's right. I have to cut it off!"

Erase the connecting lines between the arm and body and draw the lines making them two separate pieces.

"Now, here's a question. If I take this cut off arm and put it on top of the body so that I can attach it, will it look all right? Are you sure? What will be wrong, Alicia? That's right. The arm will be too short!"

If you feel at ease drawing, erase the cut off arm and redraw it on top of the body.

"Since that won't work, let's try something else. Take the cut off arm and use it as a pattern to draw the arm over again. Then, at the place where you cut it off, make the arm longer. And wider and rounder, too. You'll be punching a hole through that part of the arm. If it's skinny, what's going to happen? Right. It could fall off. Another good reason for Rule number 3."

The following pages of shadow puppet patterns illustrate a number of ways to overlap and connect moving parts. (See figs. 4.20, 4.21, page 68, 4.22, page 69, and 4.23, page 70.) The same techniques can be used for students' hand-drawn creations. After this assembly, the previous section's directions for control rods, decoration, and screen and projector operation can be followed.

(Text continues on page 71.)

Fig. 4.20.

Fig. 4.21.

Fig. 4.22.

From *Worlds of Shadow.* © 1996. Teacher Ideas Press. (800) 237-6124.

5

Simple Projected Scenery (Ages Three to Seven)

The projected scenery techniques in this chapter require little or no art skills, use the most common and inexpensive materials, and take the least time to create. But make no mistake—even the most talented artist would have difficulty duplicating these effects in any other fashion. They're grouped at a primary age level only because of their simplicity and accessibility; all of the visuals are suitable for older students as well.

The excitement generated by the demonstration of these effects really primes students for working on a shadow show, so it's worthwhile to familiarize yourself with them first. You may want to present individual techniques separately over a period of several days or assemble the ones you find most effective and appropriate into one presentation. Again, the italicized text is suggested narrative that can be modified for individual expression and the age and needs of your class.

PROJECTED SCENERY NEEDING NO ART SKILLS

If the students are very young, it might be worthwhile to gather up a sheet of construction paper, a clear transparency, clear pieces of colored plastic, and a bit of wax paper to quickly review and demonstrate the concepts of opacity, transparency, and translucence. (See Chapter 3, Activities 4, 5, and 6.) If the children are older or remember the concepts well, then proceed to demonstrating projected scenery.

"Do you remember how I put my hand on the projector and made its shadow really big? Good! And do you remember how you put shadow puppets on the projector and made their shadows big? Excellent!

"Right now, we put our shadow puppets on a plain white screen. But there's no scenery. There's no ground or sky or trees to make things more interesting. Would you like to make some scenery? Good. It's very easy to make. All we do is put things on the overhead projector."

Wax Paper Scenery Demonstration

■*Supplies*: wax paper, elephant cutout (fig. 3.10), dinosaur cutout (fig. 3.12), ship puppet with control rod (figs. 3.16 and 5.5), boy-on-sled puppet with control rod (fig. 5.7), two pine cones

Effect: Fog, Smoke, Darkness

After holding the wax paper behind the screen, place it on the projection stage of the overhead projector. (See fig. 5.1.)

Fig. 5.1.

"When wax paper is behind the screen, it looks gray. When you put it on the projector, it still looks gray. But now it covers the whole screen. What could this gray be? What could it be as scenery? That's right! It could be a cloudy sky . . . or fog. Perhaps smoke or nighttime or the darkness of a cave."

Effect: Ground

Move the wax paper halfway down the projection stage. (See fig. 5.2.) Be ready to move the elephant cutout across it.

Fig. 5.2.

"If you move the wax paper halfway down, then you get . . . what? Yes, it could be ground. Well, if it's ground, then something can walk on it."

Move the elephant cutout across the projection stage with appropriate noises. Please note that the elephant doesn't have to walk on the edge of the wax paper. Moving the figure below the edge allows the wax paper to be a horizon. (Besides, then your fingers don't show.)

Effect: Hill

Now, slant the wax paper to one side. (See fig. 5.3.) Be ready to move the dinosaur cutout down the slant.

Fig. 5.3.

"What do we have now? Right! A hill. Something can walk down that, too!"

Move the dinosaur cutout down the slant with more appropriate noises.

Effect: Earthquake

Bring the wax paper level at the halfway point and move it quickly up and down. (See fig. 5.4.)

Fig. 5.4.

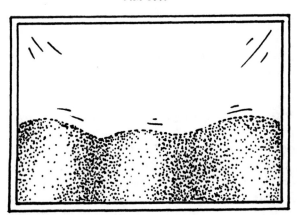

"What if I move it quickly up and down? What now? Earthquake!"

Effect: Sea

Keep the wax paper level and move it slowly from side to side. (See fig. 5.5.) Be ready to enter the ship puppet from the side of the projection stage.

Fig. 5.5.

"And if I move it slowly from side to side? The sea . . ."

Enter the ship puppet, sail it across the projection stage, and bump it into the opposite side. Tip the ship's bow up, then sink it out of sight by moving it down the projection stage.

"Actually, there are two ways to sink this ship. The first is to move the ship down like I just did. The other way is to move the water up."

Once more, sail the ship across the stage and make it bump into the opposite side. Tip the bow up, but this time slide the wax paper upward. When the screen turns entirely gray, stop sliding the wax paper and move the ship downward out of sight.

The ship can be "refloated" by reversing the process.

Effect: Snowy Ground

Now, slide the wax paper halfway up the stage. (See fig. 5.6.) Have two pine cones ready to place on the projection stage.

Fig. 5.6.

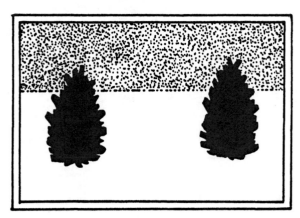

"What do we have now? Yes, we have gray sky again. But if the sky is up here, then what's down below? That's right! Ground! It's white, though. So the ground must be covered with . . . what? Snow!

"The wax paper looks like gray sky, and where there's nothing on the overhead it looks like white snow. Now, I'll add these pine trees. Are they really pine trees, though? No, they're pine cones! But they look like pine trees growing out of the snow."

Effect: Snowy Hill

Take off the pine cones, tilt the wax paper, and be ready to bring the boy-on-sled puppet down the slant. (See fig. 5.7.)

Fig. 5.7.

"We have a snowy hill! What do you do down a snowy hill? You sled!"

Bring the boy-on-sled puppet down the slant.

Effect: Cracked Glass, Broken Rock, Spider Web

Crumple the wax paper into a ball and flatten it out again on the projection stage. (See fig. 5.8.) Link your thumbs and spread your fingers to imitate a spider on the wax paper.

Fig. 5.8.

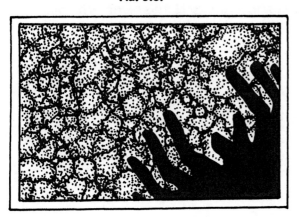

"When I crumple up the wax paper, all the wax on the paper gets cracked. Then it looks like this. What could it be? Cracked glass or broken rock. Maybe a spider web. Look out! Here comes the spider!"

Move your spidery hands onto the crumpled wax paper and back out again.

Effect: Pathway

Zigzag the wax paper in half and separate it slightly. (See fig. 5.9.) The resulting white space can be a pathway for shadow puppets.

Fig. 5.9.

Effect: Mountains and Hills

Place one-half of the wax paper on top of the other with the zigzags uppermost. (See fig. 5.10.)

Fig. 5.10.

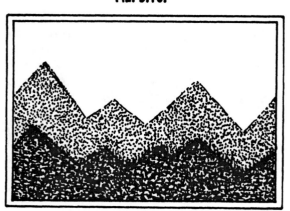

"And what do we have now? That's right! Mountains and hills! One little piece of wax paper made all that scenery."

Clear Colored Plastic Scenery Demonstration

■*Supplies*: squares of blue, red, and yellow transparent plastic measuring approximately 4" x 6", clear tape

Fig. 5.11.

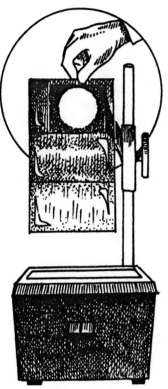

We first used clear colored plastic to demonstrate transparency against the shadow screen (Chapter 3, Activity 5). Now that the material will be used in front of the lens of the overhead projector, the clarity of the plastic and its heat resistance have to be considered.

The least effective material is gift-wrap cellophane. Its colors become hazy and faded when projected. The colored plastic sheets available in office supply stores project better color but are not heat resistant. Though they are fine for this demonstration, don't keep them in front of the lens for any length of time. The projector's focused light can burn holes in them.

The best choice is Roscolux, as it provides a wide variety of clear colors and is designed to withstand the heat of stage lights. As mentioned in Chapter 3, a free swatchbook of this theater gel is available, so request one when ordering RoscoScreen Twin-White. The sample sheets measure only 1¾" x 4", but they're adequate for the demonstration.

If you'd like to work with larger stock, Roscolux sheets are available in 20"-x-24" sheets for $5.50 each. Before ordering them, check with the drama teacher of your local high school or college or the technical director of a community theater to see if they have any leftover sheets or remnants. Because they cut much larger sections for their lighting instruments, what they discard as scrap is usually more than enough for projected scenery.

Cut 4"-x-6" rectangles of blue, red, and yellow plastic and butt them together in that order using clear tape. If working with swatchbook samples, tape two similar shades of each color together. (See fig. 5.11.)

Fig. 5.12.

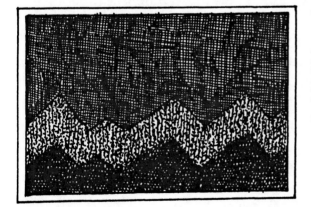

Effect: Nighttime

With the wax paper mountains still in place from the previous activity, hold the strip of colors behind the screen first. Then move the colors back to the projector, putting the top blue section in front of the lens. (See fig. 5.12.)

"We can add colored plastic to color the sky in this scene. We don't need big pieces because the plastic doesn't go on the big glass stage of the projector. Instead, you hold it in front of the lens where the light comes out. That way, the light goes through the plastic and colors the whole screen.

"We'll start with the blue first. What time of day do you think it will look like? Yes, it looks like nighttime. But if you want it to look like morning . . ."

Effect: Sunrise and Sunset

Raise the strip slowly. As the red plastic enters the light, a graduated blend of blue and red appears on the screen. (See fig. 5.13.) Continue raising the strip to yellow, and the same blending will occur with red and yellow. Stop when the screen is entirely yellow.

Fig. 5.13.

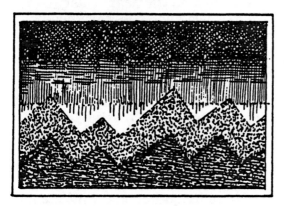

"See, it looks like the sun rising. If you want a sunset, just go the other way."

Slowly lower the strip back to blue.

Effect: Volcanic Eruptions

While moving the wax paper mountains up and down with one hand, quickly raise and lower the color strip. (See fig. 5.14.) Move between blue and red first; then raise to yellow as the eruption gets more violent. Students love sound effects with this visual, by the way.

Fig. 5.14.

"Look out! The sky is flashing red. That's right! I think a volcano is going to blow its top! KA-BLOOEY!"

Fig. 5.15.

Effect: Rocket Blastoff

You can achieve other effects by varying the colors in the strip. For instance, a strip of red and yellow can accompany the blastoff of a rocket ship on the projection stage. (The rocket ship can be used against the screen, but the puppeteer has to stand to the side in order to raise it. This isn't a problem, but the audience seeing a paper rocket ship float above the shadow screen is.)

Cut out a copy of the accompanying rocket ship from poster paper and put a control rod on it. (See fig. 5.15.) Place the rocket on the projection stage and hold the control rod upward and to the side. As the engine ignites, flash the clear yellow plastic in front of the overhead lens. Move the rocket ship up the projection stage as you move the color strip into red. When the rocket rises out of sight, move the red plastic upward from the overhead lens, too.

"Let's have a countdown to blastoff. 5. . . 4. . . 3. . . 2. . . 1! Ignition and blastoff! It looks good, Houston!"

Effect: Magic Powers

A strip of clear green plastic moved sideways across the lens can represent a magic spell cast by a puppet or student shadow against the screen. (See fig. 5.16.)

Fig. 5.16.

"Who would like to make all the green beans in the cafeteria disappear? I knew it! Just about everybody. Lynn, please come behind the screen and move your hands mysteriously back and forth. Oooh, look! Nothing can stop the power of Lynn!"

When trying this last effect, note that image reversal doesn't occur in front of the lens. It happens only on the projection stage.

Lace and Paper Doily Scenery Demonstration

■*Supplies*: a yard or two of lace material about 18" wide, one paper doily

Before purchasing lace or casement fabric, examine the pattern and consider what the projection of it might be used for. The floral designs of lace can become gardens, forests, and jungles; the square weaves of casement fabric can be used for anything from fishing nets to the windowed sides of skyscrapers.

Effect: Fancy Backgrounds

Begin with a paper doily held against the screen, then centered on the projection stage of the overhead projector. (See fig. 5.17.)

Fig. 5.17.

"This fancy piece of paper is called a doily. People sometimes put them under birthday cakes or on the dinner table to dress things up. The nice thing about doilies is that the holes are already cut out. When you put one on the projector, all the little holes look a lot bigger. See? Now what could it be? A decorated ceiling, perhaps, or one of those big cloth tapestries hanging in a king's throne room."

Effect: Hill with Flowers

Move the doily halfway down the projection stage. (See fig. 5.18.) This can be an effective backdrop for "Jack and Jill" in Chapter 6.

Fig. 5.18.

"*Yes, now it could be a hill filled with summer flowers. Very good!*"

Effect: Horizontal Moving Scenery (Joggers)

Unfold the length of lace and hold it against the screen. Then place the lace from side to side on the projection stage so that you can pull it toward you. (See fig. 5.19.)

Fig. 5.19.

"*Lace is a special fabric used mainly for curtains and table cloths, but we can use it on the overhead projector, too. Like the doily, the pattern of holes resembles flowers in a garden. But the lace is a long piece of cloth, so you can move it back and forth on the projector. Then it looks like moving scenery up on the screen. To demonstrate this, I need one person to run in place behind the screen.*"

Select a student to come behind the screen and cast a shadow in profile. Because of image reversal, the student must face in the same direction that you pull the lace. If your volunteer is very young, make sure that he or she knows what "running in place" means. (We've had at least three occasions when volunteers ran out into the hall.)

"Thank you for your help, Ling. Keep facing that way and get ready to run in place. Don't really run or you'll end up out on the playground. Just pretend that you're running while standing in one place. At the count of three? One . . . two . . . three!"

Pull the lace toward you on the overhead at a moderate speed. The effect is of scenery passing as the jogger runs. Stop when you get near the end of the lace; then step to the other side of the projector. Get ready to pull the lace more quickly.

"That's great, Ling! Now turn around and get ready to run in place much faster. Here we go! Run!"

Pull the lace quickly across the projection stage until it's gone.

"Thank you, Ling. Wow! I've never seen anybody run that fast before."

Effect: Vertical Moving Scenery (Superhero Saves the Day!)

The lace can move vertically as well as horizontally. Place the lace on the projector so that it's halfway up the projection stage with the rest of the fabric draped off the front of the machine. (See fig. 5.20.) Check that the lace won't get caught on the projector's knobs or switches.

Choose two students to come backstage.

Fig. 5.20.

"If the lace can move from side to side, it can move up and down, too. For this demonstration, I need one person to be a superhero and another person to be rescued after falling off a building.

"Kadeem, you be the person on the roof of this very tall building. A big gust of wind will come along and blow you off. That's when I'll move the lace so that it looks like you're falling. Remember to wave your arms around, too.

"Monica, you're Superwoman. After Kadeem's fallen for a few moments, you come in and grab him by the wrist. That's when I'll stop moving the lace. When you raise one arm to fly Kadeem back up to the roof, I'll move the lace the other way.

"Class, I want you to make the wind noise . . . now! Kadeem, start falling!"

Standing behind the overhead projector, pull the lace toward you. Stop when Superwoman makes the rescue. Step to the side of the projector and pull the lace down the projection stage until it reaches the end.

"What a rescue! That was terrific!"

It's happened that we've sometimes chosen boys who would rather keep on falling than be rescued by a girl. In one case, a Superman just let go of a Lois Lane and flew off the screen. If budding chauvinism interferes with the activity that badly, then use two girls or two boys in the roles.

Natural Materials Scenery Demonstration

■*Supplies*: flowers, weeds, grass, elephant cutout (fig. 3.10), a leafy twig about 2' long, roll of masking tape

Because flowers, weeds, and grass have distinctive shapes, they can be magnified on the overhead projector and still be recognized. Whether the setting is a cultivated garden or a wild jungle depends on how much vegetation you place on the projector.

Effect: Weeding the Garden

Begin by identifying plants one at a time to the students out front. Then hold each one behind the screen before placing it on the projection stage. (See fig. 5.21.)

Fig. 5.21.

> *"This pink flower is called a carnation. When I hold it behind the screen, you can see how round its shadow is. Now I'll put it on the overhead projector.*
>
> *"This rose has something the carnation doesn't. That's right! It has sharp thorns. You can see them when I hold the rose behind the screen, but they show up better on the projector.*
>
> *"I'm sure you've seen dandelions in the garden. How do you know this is a dandelion? Yes, it has a fuzzy puffball of seeds. Is the dandelion something we want in the garden? No, it's a weed. I'll put it carefully on the projector once you've seen its shadow behind the screen.*
>
> *"And this long stuff is grass. It's nice to have on the lawn, but do we want grass growing in the garden? No way! But it's in there now."*

Select a student to come behind the screen and walk through this giant unkempt garden. When the student points out a plant that doesn't belong, pluck it off the projection stage.

A funny alternative is to let the student do the heavy work.

> *"Alex, this flower garden seems to have a lot of weeds and grass growing in it. Would you walk through it and pull out the things that don't belong? That's right. Grab hold of that weed and pull!"*

When the student pulls the projected shadow of the weed, jerk the actual weed on the projection stage. Work with the motions of the student. After the weed is uprooted, move it off the projector as if it's falling. When the garden is cleared, other students can be invited behind the screen to smell the giant flowers.

"Thank you, Alex. That was a tremendous amount of work. Why don't you rest a moment? Here come Amy and Colin to walk through the garden and smell the flowers. Could you tell us the names of these flowers?"

Effect: Wild Jungle

Add more vegetation to the previous scene; then invite a student to explore the wild jungle created on the shadow screen. Note that the student shadow against the screen is darker than the projected shadow of the plants. (See fig. 5.22.)

Fig. 5.22.

Hold the tricolored plastic used for sunrises and sunsets (fig. 5.11) in front of the projector's lens to make it nighttime in the jungle. Get ready to enter the elephant cutout. (Unless you want the elephant to tromp on the plants and knock them out of the way, keep the cutout slightly elevated above the projection stage.)

"The great explorer Christine is lost in the jungle. Uh-oh! Night is falling! That's no time to be lost in the jungle. What's going to happen? Wait a minute . . .

Shake the projector gently with the approach of heavy elephant footsteps. Enter the elephant cutout from the side of the projection stage. For a happy ending, have the student get on the elephant's back and ride off (as in Chapter 3, Activity 8).

"Something's coming! It's . . . it's an elephant! But it's a friendly elephant. Look! He's kneeling down. Get on his back, Christine, and you can ride away. Hold on tight!"

Effect: Growing Things ("Jack and the Beanstalk")

The two-foot leafy twig is for telling the entire story of "Jack and the Beanstalk." (If a real twig isn't handy, craft stores often sell fake greenery that can be taped together.) The student who plays Jack (or Jacqueline) has two lines to say, so this will be your first minimal brush with rehearsal. The progression of the story is detailed in figure 5.23, page 86.

"Here is a leafy twig from outdoors. With it, we can tell the entire story of 'Jack and the Beanstalk,' or maybe 'Jacqueline and the Beanstalk.' It depends on who plays the part. Robert, would you like to do it? Good! This masking tape will be your magic bean.

"You have two things to say, Robert. The first is, 'Dad! Dad! I sold the cow!' Say that back to me one time . . . fine! Then I'll say, 'What did you get for selling our cow?' Hold up the tape and say, 'This magic bean!'

"Would you like to rehearse one time?"

Fig. 5.23

Run through the lines if necessary, then place the student behind the screen. Introduce the student so he can say the first line. Remember to step briefly behind the screen to play Dad for two lines.

Teacher (narrating):	*"Jack came home from the marketplace very excited."*
Jack (excited):	*"Dad! Dad! I sold the cow!"*
Teacher (entering):	*"What did you get for selling our cow?"*
Jack (holding tape):	*"This magic bean!"*
Teacher (shocked):	*"You sold our cow for a magic bean? That's a terrible decision! I'm going to go to bed!" (exits)*
Teacher (narrating):	*"At first, Jack was upset that his Dad was so angry."*
Jack (crying):	*"Boo hoo hoo!"*
Teacher (narrating):	*"But then he decided to see if the magic bean would work. He buried it in the ground. All of a sudden, the ground began to tremble!"*

As soon as the student "plants" the masking tape below the shadow screen, move promptly to the projector and gently shake it. Place the leafy twig at the bottom of the projection stage and move it up quickly to midscreen. Voila!—the beanstalk has sprouted! Then continue moving the beanstalk up the projection stage. Stop before your fingers show.

Teacher (narrating):	*"Jack grabbed hold of the beanstalk with both hands and climbed it hand over hand!"*

The student should grasp the magnified shadow of the beanstalk on the shadow screen. (If younger children look confused or start over to the projector, a quick nod or whisper should be enough to redirect their attention to the shadow on the screen.)

When the student starts climbing, reverse the twig's direction. Stop when the end of the twig comes into view.

Teacher (narrating):	*"When Jack reached the top, he looked all around. All of a sudden, heavy footsteps approached. THUD! THUD! THUD!"*

Shake the twig with each footstep. Then place your hand on the projection stage and reach toward Jack with your magnified hand shadow. For a laugh, scratch Jack's head with your giant finger.

Teacher (narrating):	*"It was the giant! Jack climbed down the beanstalk as fast as he could!"*

Again, move the twig up the projection stage as the student descends.

| Teacher (narrating): | *"When he got to the bottom, he chopped the beanstalk down with his bare hands!"* |

Jerk the twig with every chop the student makes against the screen. Then let the twig fall to one side and land on the bottom of the projection stage. Another shake of the projector gives the final landing some weight.

| Teacher (narrating): | *"The end!"* |

This condensed version of the Grimm Brothers classic takes only a couple of minutes to perform and really doesn't require more rehearsal than indicated here. As long as you know your lines and actions on the projector, the students will almost always follow along. In the hundreds of times we've conducted this demonstration, only a couple of children have needed further prompting to climb or descend the beanstalk.

Water Pan Scenery Demonstration

■*Supplies*: transparent pan, water, plastic wrap, rubber band, masking tape, whale cutout (fig. 3.11), set of food colors, Alka-Seltzer or other fizzing tablet, milk, cooking oil, liquid detergent, two cups of play sand, paper towels (just in case)

When a transparent pan of water is held directly underneath the reflecting lens of the overhead projector, the motion of the water is transmitted to the screen. This is a terrific effect for underwater scenes as well as dreams, memories, and time travel. (See fig. 5.24.)

Fig. 5.24.

Pyrex baking dishes and casseroles work well for this purpose, as will any shallow transparent container whether it be circular or rectangular, plastic or glass.

Caution: Because this technique involves the use of water with electrical equipment, great care must be taken. The projection stage can be wiped dry of a few drops, but it's not watertight. For that reason, it's usually best for the teacher to handle the water pan. Unless the pan is steep-sided or contains a minimum of water, it's often wise to seal the top of it with clear plastic wrap and secure it with a rubber band. The projection stage of the overhead can also be protected with plastic wrap and secured with masking tape. Just don't cover the projector's air vents! And keep that roll of paper towels nearby, just in case.

If you lower the pan to the projection stage, the water will be projected in focus. Gently shaking and swirling the pan will result in clearly seen waves and ripples.

Make sure that there are no brand names stamped on the bottom of the pan. Audiences will have a hard time believing in an underwater world if the word "PYREX*" is emblazoned across the screen. This can be avoided by using the flat-bottomed glass lid of some casseroles or by using generic brands.

Also, the rim of the pan will project as a heavy black line, so try to use a dish wider than the projection stage. If this is hard to find, directions for a plexiglass pan with an optional lid follow. (See fig. 5.25.) Glass and plastics suppliers will cut the plastic to size for you, though most will probably charge extra to actually construct the pan. As always, it's cheaper to make it yourself.

Fig. 5.25.

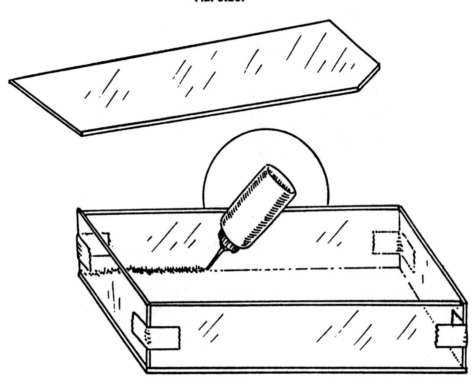

■*Supplies*: from 1/8" clear plexiglass: two 12"-x-12" pieces, two 2"-x-12" pieces, and two 2"-x-11½" pieces; plexiglass glue, masking tape, saber saw with plastic-cutting blade

■*Directions*: Tape four sides of pan in place on one 12"-x-12" piece. After reading safety precautions and ventilation suggestions, apply plexiglass glue along inside of all joints. The capillary action of the glue will run into the spaces between pieces and bond them. Let dry. Check for leaks.

For the optional lid, saw a 2" right triangle off one corner of the other 12"-x-12" piece of plexiglass. This will be the hole in the pan's lid for filling and emptying water. Position lid and apply glue to outside of all joints. After drying, check for leaks.

(Please note that condensation sometimes forms inside this lidded pan. To clear it, block the filler hole with the palm of your hand; then turn the pan briefly upside down. The water will clear the fogginess.)

Effect: Under Water, Dreams, Memories, Time Travel

Put in at least enough water to cover the bottom of the pan; then hold the pan directly underneath the reflecting lens. The slightest movement will ripple the water, creating diffuse undulations on the shadow screen. (See fig. 5.26.)

Select a student to operate the whale cutout on the projector.

Fig. 5.26.

"Maria, would you help me by operating this whale on the projector? Thank you. Now, I'm going to hold this clear pan of water underneath the lens of the overhead projector. I'm going to do it very slowly so that I don't spill it.

"There! Now, can everybody see the water move? Good!

"Maria, would you move the whale on the projector now?"

Effect: Water Level (Calm or Stormy Seas)

If the pan is lidded and definitely watertight, it can be tilted slightly while on the projection stage to create a water level on the shadow screen. (See fig. 5.27.) Shadow puppet ships, sea creatures, and the students' own swimming shadows can easily be used in conjunction with this effect, but only against the shadow screen. (The water pan precludes any figure use on the overhead projector.)

For stormy seas, simply shake the tilted water pan.

Fig. 5.27.

Effect: Primary Colors and Secondary Colors

If the water is in focus, anything added to the water will be in focus, too. Of course, that means an uncovered pan, so please be careful.

Uncap the containers of yellow, blue, and red food coloring. Start with three or four drops of yellow, followed by a few drops of blue. (See fig. 5.28.) After demonstrating how these primary colors produce green, add more yellow to a clear area. A drop or two of red will create orange. If necessary, change the water before showing how red and blue make purple.

Fig. 5.28.

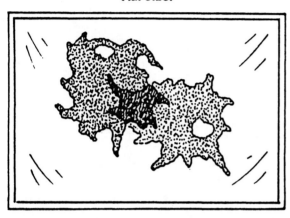

"Yellow, red, and blue are called primary colors. Primary means 'first,' like Dana when she's first in line. When you mix any two of these primary colors together, you get secondary colors. Let's find out what they are.

"When I mix yellow and blue, I get . . . what? That's right! Green.

"And when I mix yellow and red? Orange!

"How about blue and red? Purple!"

Effect: Water Pollution, Intergalactic Clouds

Gently swirl the multicolored drops of food coloring. For outer space, add a piece of clear blue plastic in front of the projector's lens to color the entire scene. (See fig. 5.29.)

Fig. 5.29.

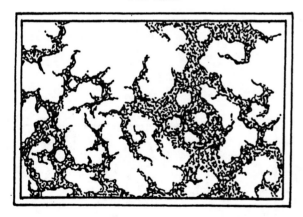

Effect: Exploding Planets

Add an Alka-Seltzer or other fizzing tablet to the water. Food coloring in the pan and colored plastic in front of the lens enhance the effect. (See fig. 5.30.)

Fig. 5.30.

Effect: Black Clouds

Pouring milk into the water creates voluminous black clouds that billow across the shadow screen. Besides creating thunderstorms, this effect can be used to blank out a scene prior to changing it. (See fig. 5.31.)

Fig. 5.31.

Effect: Globules

A dollop of cooking oil will break into scores of little globules when swizzled with a straw or stirring stick, then will quickly rejoin. (See fig. 5.32.) For continued water movement, use a turkey baster to jet water in from the side of the pan.

Fig. 5.32.

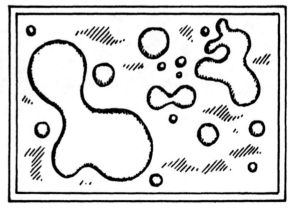

Effect: Bubbles

Add a squirt or two of liquid dishwashing detergent to the water and blow into it with a straw. The resulting bubbles will be projected on the screen. (See fig. 5.33.)

Fig. 5.33.

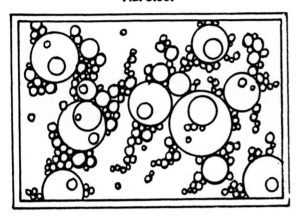

Effect: Appearing Letters

Thoroughly dry the pan before adding a cupful of play sand. Spread it evenly over the surface of the pan and place it on the overhead projector. Add more sand if any light seeps through.

When you write on the sand with a fingertip or pencil eraser, bear down hard enough to clear the sand from the bottom of the pan. The projected letters will magically appear on the shadow screen. (See fig. 5.34.) Remember, you'll have to write *backward* because of image reversal!

Fig. 5.34.

Construction Paper Scenery Demonstration

■*Supplies*: construction paper, scissors

Although intricate pieces of scenery can certainly be cut from construction paper, these effects use whole sheets or minimal cutting.

Effect: Ground (Hills and Mountains)

As with the wax paper, positioning the construction paper halfway up the projection stage results in a ground level. Because the projected shadow is black instead of gray, however, shadow characters have to walk right on the ground level. (See fig. 5.35.) Cutting or tearing the edge creates hills and mountains.

Fig. 5.35.

Effect: Walls, Sides of Buildings

Placing the side of a piece of construction paper vertically on the projection stage results in a wall or side of a building. That is not very exciting, but if the top of the paper is positioned so that it shows on the screen and the paper is then moved, it provides a simple backdrop for the misadventures of Humpty-Dumpty in Chapter 6. (See fig. 5.36.)

Fig. 5.36.

Effect: Tunnels (Digging Them Out and Filling Them In)

Cut or tear a long narrow section out of the middle of a piece of construction paper. Place the construction paper (not the torn-out piece) on the projector. This negative space will be the tunnel. (See fig. 5.37.)

After cutting or tearing the edge of another piece of construction paper, place it over the tunnel, covering it completely. As shadow puppet characters dig a tunnel on the screen or the projection stage, slowly move the cover sheet back to expose the tunnel. Reverse the process to fill it in.

Fig. 5.37.

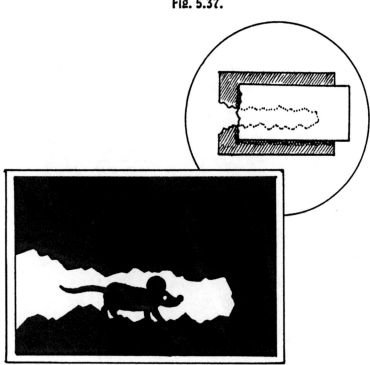

Effect: Lightning

Draw two or three lightning bolts on a piece of construction paper; then cut them out and throw them away. Place the paper with the lightning bolt holes on the overhead projector. Instead of turning the projector on and off to make the lightning flash, hold a piece of cardboard in front of the lens and move it quickly. (See fig. 5.38.) Remember, lightning spends more time off than on. To color the bolts, tape a piece of yellow or orange clear plastic in front of the reflecting lens.

Fig. 5.38.

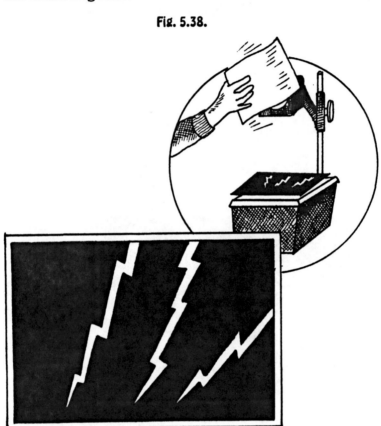

Effect: Moving Eyes

Cut two eyeholes out of a piece of construction paper; then place a transparency over it. Draw or stick two small circles on the transparency, one "pupil" over each eyehole. On the projector, keep the eyeholes still while sliding the transparency back and forth or up and down. (See fig. 5.39.)

To make the eyes blink, lower a strip of construction paper over them from the top. For a wink, slide the paper over one eye.

Fig. 5.39.

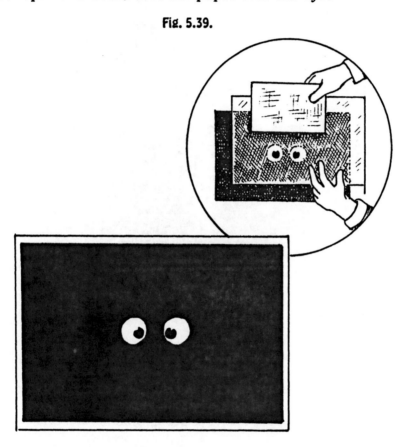

Effect: Moving Mouth

Cut the upper jaw of a mouth (and other facial features) out of a piece of construction paper. Cut the lower jaw from another piece, lay it on top of the other, and slide it up and down for speaking or eating. (See fig. 5.40.)

Fig. 5.40.

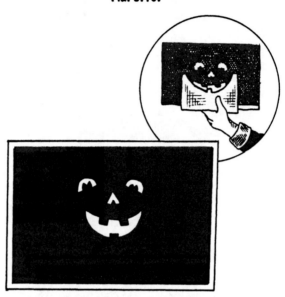

Art Tissue Scenery Demonstration

■*Supplies*: art tissue, scissors

Although art tissue paper is visually quite bright, its dense weave makes it almost devoid of color when projected. However, the tiny pinpricks of light that do get through make art tissue paper excellent for representing the next effect.

Fig. 5.41.

Effect: Interstellar Space

A sheet of blue art tissue paper laid on the overhead projector is all that's necessary, although the room has to be quite dark for this effect to look its best. Cutting in small stars and moons adds to the illusion. (See fig. 5.41.)

Patterned Plexiglass Scenery Demonstration

■*Supplies*: sheets of patterned plexiglass measuring at least 8" x 10"

Plastic suppliers often have waste bins or marked-down remnants of patterned plexiglass that can yield some interesting (and economical) visuals.

Effect: Fog

The wavy-patterned plexiglass used for shower doors and picnic tables makes an excellent mist and fog effect. The distortion is greatest when the plastic is held underneath the reflecting lens of the projector and gradually becomes clearer as it's lowered to the projection stage. (See fig. 5.42.)

Fig. 5.42.

Effect: Changing Patterns

The clear, ridged plastic used to cover fluorescent lights changes patterns much like a kaleidoscope when it's lowered from the reflecting lens (upper portion of fig. 5.43) to the projection stage (lower portion of same).

Fig. 5.43.

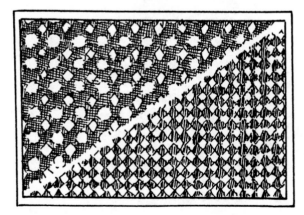

Effect: Grids (Honeycomb, Skyscraper Windows, and Background Patterns)

Plastic light grids come in tiny squares, rectangles, and hexagons, supplying ready-made patterns for beehives, the sides of skyscrapers, or any other locale demanding a repeated design. (See fig. 5.44.)

Fig. 5.44.

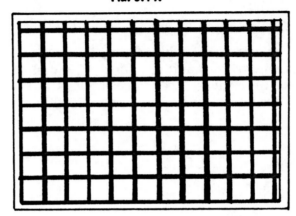

PROJECTED SCENERY NEEDING MINIMAL ART SKILLS

All of the previous effects involved putting one or two things on the overhead projector to achieve screenwide backgrounds for an extended period of time. But what if you need a scene with a number of details such as the furniture of a room or the trees of a forest? And what if you need to change scenes promptly?

Instead of laboriously placing each element on the projector (and just as laboriously picking it off, all accompanied by the giant shadow of your hand), mount such scenes on 8½"-x-11" transparencies. Then all the scenery moves on and off the projector with the transparency quickly and easily. (See fig. 5.45.)

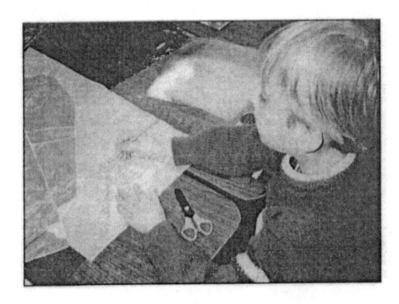

Fig. 5.45.

Media Choices for Black-and-White Transparency Scenery

1. *Transparency ink pens:* Various brands of overhead projector pens are available for drawing scenes on transparencies. Younger artists will need to be cautioned that the ink of some brands doesn't dry instantly. (Left-handers especially will have to watch out for smudging their work.) To avoid messy mistakes with black permanent ink, try penciling the scene on typing paper first, then laying the transparency over it and tracing. The only drawback to ink is that you see individual black lines rather than the complete shadow offered by the following alternatives.

2. *Cut paper:* Typing paper, lined notebook paper, or thin construction paper are perfectly adequate for cutting out scenery pieces. To attach them, use dry adhesives such as double-stick tape or double-stick photo mountings rather than glue sticks or paste, which can produce highly visible smears.

3. *Self-adhesive contact paper:* This material has the advantage of having the adhesive already in place. Black or dark contact papers tend to absorb heat from the overhead projector and shrink, so pick a plain white or light color. Draw and cut the scenery pieces before peeling off the backing paper. Be careful how you place them on the transparency, though, as the adhesive is unforgiving. Any air bubbles can be rubbed out or pricked with a pin and flattened.

4. *Gloss opaque Form-X film (Series 30000):* Similar to contact paper, this opaque, self-adhesive film is also heat resistant. Again, it's better to use white or ivory, the next lightest color. It can be ordered from a good art supply store or directly from the manufacturer: Graphic Products Corporation, 1480 South Wolf Road, Wheeling, IL 60090 (Tel. 708-537-9300, Fax: 708-215-0111). Sheets measuring 20" x 26" cost about $5.25 each. Larger rolls are also available: 20"-x-15" rolls cost $25, and 40" x 18" rolls cost $53.50. The company will send a free catalog and current price sheet upon request.

5. *Scenes for copying on transparencies:* This book contains a number of scenes ready for transfer to transparency. (Coloring books might also offer some usable material.)

Media Choices for Color Transparency Scenery

1. *Transparency ink pens:* Again, individual lines will be seen rather than solid color. But the colors transmit well and are especially useful for coloring black-and-white scenes copied to transparencies.

2. *Acetate inks:* Applied with brushes, these colors combine nicely to create evocative swirls, but we'd hesitate to use them for detailed work.

3. *Theater gel:* The heat-resistant colors of Roscolux look wonderful but lack adhesive to stick them to transparencies. Unfortunately, glue or clear tape shows badly when projected.

4. *Gloss transparent Form-X film (Series 10000):* Available in seventeen colors that can be overlapped to create new or intensified shades (as illustrated in the catalog), this is an excellent heat-resistant color medium. Again, it is cut, peeled, and applied like contact paper. Its size formats and prices are identical to the gloss opaque variety. This product has been our consistent choice for color scenery.

Differing Densities of Projected Shadows and Screen Shadows

It's usually advisable that scenes contain a fair amount of white or colored space for clear viewing of shadow puppets. If students construct a scene with a lot of black area, it's still all right for shadow puppets operated against the screen. Their shadows are always darker than projected shadows. (See fig. 5.22.)

However, the scene's black areas could cause visibility problems for figures operated on the overhead projector, as their shadows will have the same density. (See fig. 5.46.) If such is the case, dark scenes can usually be "opened up" by slimming down details with scissors or a teacher-manipulated X-Acto knife.

Fig. 5.46.

"Edged" Scenery

The opposite problem occurs when students place scenery on the very edges of a transparency. (See fig. 5.47.) The overhead projector's square stage can't accommodate both sides of the rectangular transparency, so the big empty space in the middle usually gets projected. Also, the thin strip of scenery at the bottom is incredibly difficult to align with the bottom of the screen.

Fig. 5.47.

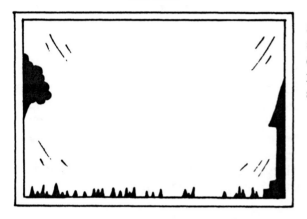

Let your students know that they can fill a transparency with scenery and still see the shadow puppets. If children have already created "edged" scenery, it's usually possible for them to add more details to expand the sides and bottom.

Relative Scale Between Projected Image and Screen Shadow Puppets

The relative scale between projected scenery and figures operated against the shadow screen isn't critical when the setting is a general one, for example, a forest or outer space. But once a shadow puppet has to interact with a detail of projected scenery (such as sitting on a park bench or entering a rocket ship's air lock), the issue becomes more important. (See fig. 5.48.)

Fig. 5.48.

Or does it? We've overseen many student productions where the hero had to stand on a chair to reach the table he was sitting at, the limousine was smaller than the chauffeur driving it, and the fly was bigger than the head of the old lady who purportedly swallowed it. None of these anomalies bothered the performers or their audiences. (In fact, they were often the most charming and hilarious parts of the show for all concerned.)

As with the first-grader's initial effort at drawing a pig in figure 4.16, it's often better to let these disproportionate moments pass by without subjecting them to adult critique—unless, of course, the students notice them and decide they should be addressed. Then action must be taken, for these self-aware students would rather do the corrective work than appear foolish or immature in performance.

Explaining Relative Scale

Explaining and demonstrating relative scale prior to construction saves time-consuming problem solving later on. Prepare a transparency with the length and width marked off in inches. (See fig. 5.49.) Place it on the overhead projector backward. (Remember image reversal!) Get ready to place a 10"-12"-tall shadow puppet against the screen.

The narrative offered here is in the context of "Little Red Riding Hood." Feel free to adapt an instance from the story you're working on.

Fig. 5.49.

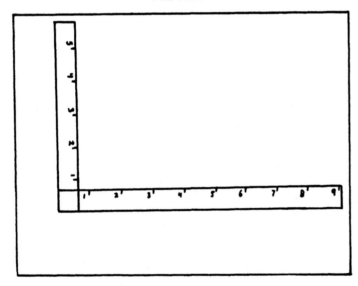

"*Before we begin making puppets and scenery, let's take a look at something. I've marked off this transparency in inches, just like your rulers. Now I'll put it on the overhead projector. Wow! See how big just one inch becomes when we project it on the screen? This is important to remember when we put our show together.*

"*In this story about Red Riding Hood, the wolf is in bed disguised as Grandma. Let's pretend this shadow puppet is the wolf. I'll lay him out flat along the line of inches. There! How many inches long should the bed be? That's right! Only four inches! Maybe five if it's king-size.*

"*Now we'll see how tall the bed should be. I'll raise the shadow puppet until my hands begin to show. It looks like the bed can't be any taller than three inches.*

"*Anytime you guys wonder how big to make a part of the scenery, come and get this transparency with the inch marks and we'll figure it out.*"

When using this technique for correcting relative scale, you must use the same overhead projector and shadow screen setup throughout rehearsal and performance. Changing to a differently lensed machine or a larger shadow screen will throw the scale off.

Exploring Placement

Solving a relative-scale problem when everything is already made is more difficult (and sometimes unsuccessful). If a shadow puppet is far too small for a detail of projected scenery, try putting the puppet on the projector, too. As a close-up, the enlarged shadow might work better. If the size discrepancy is less grievous, hold the figure a few inches back from the shadow screen to increase the shadow size.

If neither option works, try the following.

Making It Over

Alas, the final option is sometimes a necessary one. If the problem lies with the projected scenery, identify the problem detail and correct only that section rather than trashing the entire transparency. If the size discrepancy lies with the shadow puppet, see if a portion of the figure can be shortened, lengthened, or replaced before constructing a new puppet.

Changing Transparency Scenes

Sliding scenes on and off the overhead projector exposes transparency edges as well as the fingers and thumbs of those changing the scenes, a real challenge to your audience's willing suspension of disbelief.

It's much better to lift a transparency scene straight up to the reflecting lens of the projector. (See fig. 5.50, page 106.) This way, the scene fades smoothly out of focus. Then slip a second scene directly underneath the lifted first one. Lower the second scene onto the projector's glass stage as you remove the first from underneath the reflecting lens. Don't rush and . . . voila! A new scene comes into focus just as smoothly. However, this genteel method of scene changing won't look half as good if the transparencies droop. Try to keep them flat as you lift and lower them.

Scenes can be mounted in paper or plastic transparency holders, but they create black blurs when crossing the light of the overhead projector. We use 12"-x-12" sheets of thin plexiglass for our shows. They're certainly clear and rigid, but at $2 or more a sheet, not something to make a lot of mistakes with.

We've now covered all the basics: light, screen, shadows, shadow puppets, and projected scenery. Some of these elements have already been used in brief skits and presentations. But now we start putting everything together into actual productions.

Fig. 5.50.

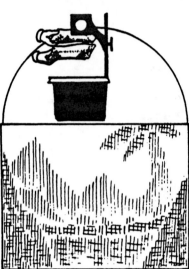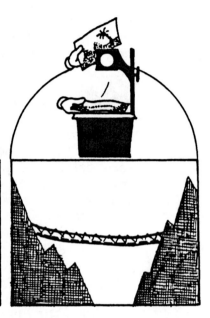

6

Production, Rehearsal, and Performance with Ages Three to Five

"Production, rehearsal and performance with three- to five-year-olds?" you might say. "Have they lost their minds?" The short answer is, "Yes, many times." Be that as it may, this process is possible if the project is kept simple, short, and very informal (keeping in mind, of course, that the process is more important than the product).

All the students can be involved in these brief productions if they're performed with multiple casts (small groups of children taking turns operating individual figures) or if the number of characters is expanded (all the children operating multiple copies of individual figures). Also, incidental characters can be added without drawing undue attention to themselves: birds and butterflies in forest scenes, for example.

The following songs, rhymes, and stories are typical of what can be achieved, especially with the older children of this age bracket.

To fit as many productions as possible into an easily handled book required quite small type, perhaps too small for scripts to be easily read when conducting rehearsals. This should not be a problem with the familiar songs and rhymes that follow, but could pose a difficulty when working with the more complicated stories. If this is the case, enlarge the scripts on a copy machine and staple them into a more legible unit.

SONGS

"Old MacDonald Had a Farm"

■*Production:* Because the children's cutting skills are still developing, teachers and aides will most likely prepare shadow puppets of the various farm animals. (See figs. 4.20 and 4.21.) Make one of each if you are using multiple casts or several of each if you are expanding the number of characters.

For the simplest projected scenery, use a sheet of wax paper for ground and a rectangle of construction paper for a barn. Cut out a smaller rectangle and tape it to the larger one for a door that opens and closes. Attach a control stick with a tape tab to the door. (See fig. 6.1.) Fasten all these elements to a transparency.

Fig. 6.1.

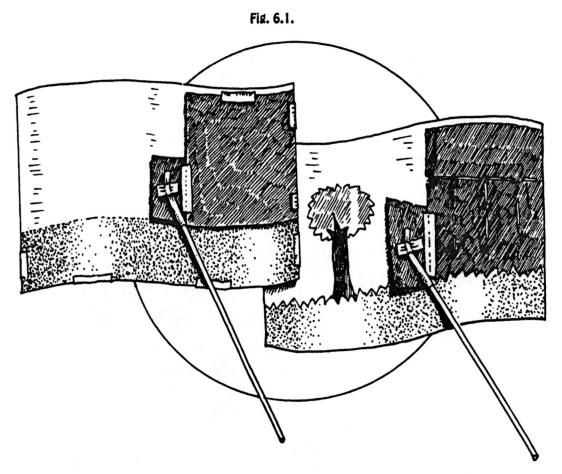

For more complex scenery, make a transparency using overhead projector pens, acetate inks, or transparent Form-X films for the ground and background trees. The barn and attached door can have color highlights but should remain largely opaque so that the shadow puppets don't show through.

The following farm scene can also be used. (See fig. 6.2.) Simply copy it to a transparency, add color, and attach a stick-controlled barn door.

Fig. 6.2.

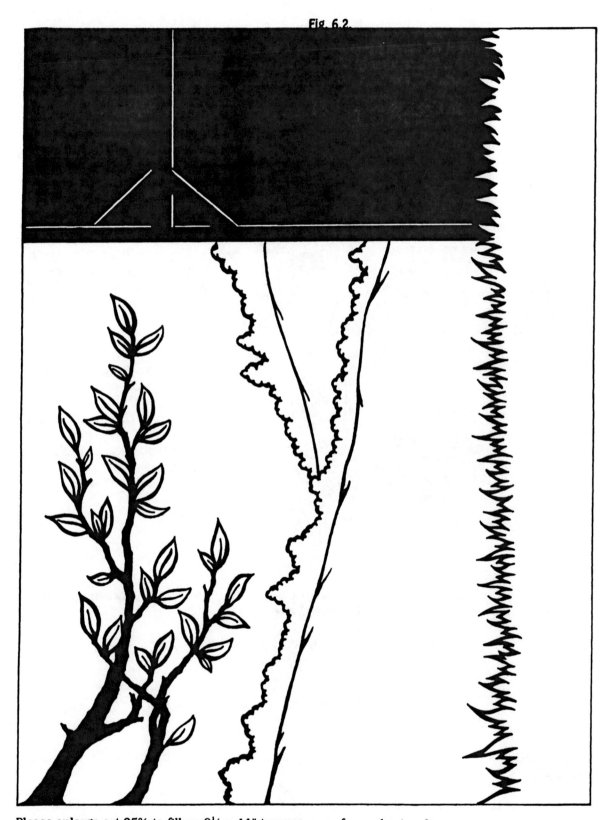

Please enlarge art 25% to fill an 8½-x-11" transparency from edge to edge.

Prepare a sunrise-sunset strip to open the show (see fig. 5.13), as well as an 8"-x-10" sheet of sturdy poster paper or cardboard to block the light from the reflecting lens. When slowly lifted and lowered, this paper provides a smooth blackout, or "curtain," for beginning and ending the program. (See fig. 6.3.)

Fig. 6.3.

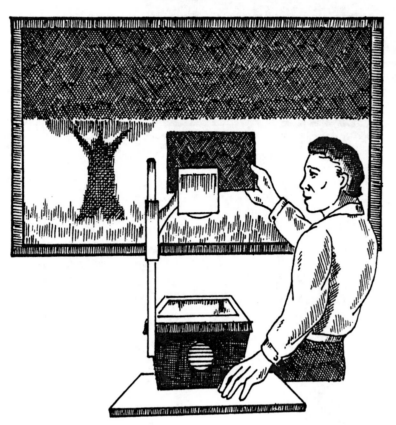

Show students the farm scene transparency; then place it on the overhead projector. If the class hasn't seen the sunrise-sunset effect, demonstrate it and then lightly tape the strip to the lens so that it's "night-time." Then display how the poster paper "curtain" is raised to start the show and lowered to end it. These three elements compose the preset.

"When actors perform a play, they make sure everything is in the right place before the curtain goes up. When we perform our song, we have to do the same thing. So we'll check our stuff right now.
"Farm scene . . . check! Sunrise and sunset . . . check! Curtain . . . check!"

Black out the scene with the poster paper "curtain"; then rotate the farm scene transparency until it's upside down.

"If we don't check everything, mistakes happen."

Lift the curtain.

"Oh my gosh! They didn't check their stuff! Quick! Lower the curtain!"

Black out the scene, correct the transparency, and reveal the farm scene again.

"That's better! We don't want that to happen to us, do we? Nope! So we'll always check this stuff—our preset—before the show begins. OK?"

■*Rehearsal:* In Chapter 4's first section ("Shadow Puppet Cutouts for Ages Three to Five"), there are a number of rules and helpful hints about shadow puppet operation ("Operation behind the shadow screen") that should be communicated and demonstrated. Once the students know these basics, distribute the figures.

Determine in which order the characters will appear (cow, horse, pig, etc.) and line up the students accordingly. If expanding the number of characters, make sure each student knows the order of appearance (Cow 1, Cow 2, Cow 3, etc.).

Check the preset. Make sure the curtain is down; then turn on the projector. After raising the curtain, do the sunrise effect while starting the song. As the characters cross the screen, open and close the barn door for each one. At this point, please don't worry about heads and hands showing or if puppets enter backward. Unless someone gets completely tangled up or desperately out of line, keep singing. When the last character enters the barn, do the sunset effect and bring down the curtain with a final "Eee-yi, eee-yi, yo."

After this first run-through, decide whether your class can handle a second one. If so, correct backward-entering puppets, students moving on "all threes," and those engrossed in gazing at their creations. (See fig. 6.4.) Don't overdo consecutive rehearsals even if enthusiastic students want to continue. Try again later, or even the next day. It's better for rehearsals to remain special and fun rather than hard work. If the show is going to be performed in the multipurpose room or gym, it's worthwhile to familiarize the children with the new setup by rehearsing there once or twice.

Fig. 6.4.

■*Performance*: Keep the performance as close to a rehearsal as possible: short, informal, and uncritical. Don't let parents or older students do a "Siskel & Ebert" on the show.

"Itsy Bitsy Spider"

■*Production*: Because this short song works better with multiple casts, prepare only four or five spider shadow puppets, either simple cutouts or with moving legs. (See fig. 4.10.)

An L-shaped piece of construction paper makes an excellent drainpipe. Attach it to the center of a transparency; then draw, paint, or apply transparent Form-X film grass at the bottom of the scene. Webs can be drawn or made of string and yarn. (See fig. 6.5.) For the rain, cut a small transparent plastic bag (the grocery store variety used for fruits and vegetables) in strips and tape it to a dowel rod or ruler. This will be held in front of the projector's reflecting lens and swayed gently back and forth. A piece of transparent yellow plastic will be the sun.

Fig. 6.5.

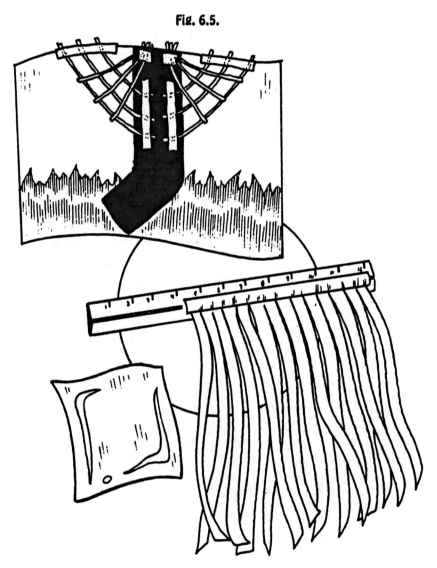

Again, the following transparency scene can be copied and colored. (See fig 6.6.)

Fig. 6.6.

Please enlarge art 25% to fill an 8½-x-11" transparency from edge to edge.

From *Worlds of Shadow.* © 1996. Teacher Ideas Press. (800) 237-6124.

■*Rehearsal:* Show the students the transparency and place it on the projector. Then demonstrate the rain and sun effects.

Distribute the shadow puppet spiders to the first cast and have them kneel behind the screen. Black out the scene with the poster paper curtain to complete the preset.

"Please don't put your puppets on the shadow screen yet. Let's first make sure our preset is in place before we start rehearsing. Waterspout scene . . . check! Rain . . . check! Sun . . . check! Puppeteers . . . check! Puppets . . . check! Curtain . . . check!
"Good. When I raise the curtain, put your spiders on the screen and move them toward the waterspout."

Raise the curtain to reveal the scene.

"Spiders enter. Good! Crawl toward the waterspout. Excellent! Now, we'll sing the song, but we'll sing it slowly so that everybody has time to move their puppets."

Itsy bitsy spiders climbed up the waterspout . . .

Bring in the rain effect.

Down came the rain and washed the spiders out . . .

The spiders exit off the bottom of the screen. Bring in the sun effect as the rain moves out. Take your time.

Up came the sun and dried up all the rain . . .

Spiders reenter and start climbing as the song ends and the curtain descends.

And the itsy bitsy spiders crawled up the spout again.

As the song is short and simple, rehearse only a few times before giving the next cast a turn.

■*Performance:* Again, keep things brief and low key.

RHYMES

"Humpty-Dumpty"

■*Production:* Cut out the figures and attach control rods. (See fig. 6.7 and 6.8, page 116.) Although only two versions of the main character are necessary, the number of king's horses and king's men (and king's women) can be expanded.

Fig. 6.7.

From *Worlds of Shadow*. © 1996. Teacher Ideas Press. (800) 237-6124.

Scenery can be as simple as a strip of construction paper or lace for Humpty-Dumpty's wall. Simply slide the material up the projection stage to give the illusion of downward movement. Previous examples of this technique are in Chapter 5, "Vertical Moving Scenery" (fig. 5.20) and "Jack and the Beanstalk" (fig. 5.23). For the hard landing, tape a length of construction paper to the bottom of the wall. (See fig. 6.9.)

Fig. 6.9.

■*Rehearsal:* After showing students how the scenery works, place it on the projector. Distribute the shadow puppets to the first cast. Direct the whole Humpty-Dumpty to sit on the projected shadow of the wall. The cracked version should stay below the shadow screen for now. The king's troops should be ready to enter on either side of the screen.

Check the preset.

"Marcus, would you please operate Humpty-Dumpty on the shadow screen? Kneel down and place him on top of the wall. Shauna, keep the other Humpty-Dumpty out of sight below the screen for right now. Evan and Kathy, keep your king's men out of sight on the sides of the screen.
"Let's check our preset. Good! Everything's in place. I'll bring the curtain down.
"Now, we'll say the rhyme together slowly. If we need to stop and start over, that's fine. That's what rehearsals are all about."

Raise the curtain.

> *Humpty-Dumpty sat on a wall.*
> *Humpty-Dumpty had a great faaallllllll . . .*

When Humpty-Dumpty tilts off the wall, move it up the projection stage. After Humpty-Dumpty bounces off the ground and falls out of sight, the cracked version should appear. His appearance will be the cue for the entrance of all the king's horses and all the king's men.

> *All the king's horses and all the king's men*
> *Couldn't put Humpty-Dumpty together again!*

Please take your time and be patient. Although the students are old enough to understand the sequence of events in this rhyme, following cues is probably a new experience.

"When Marcus makes Humpty-Dumpty tilt over, then I know it's time to make the wall move. That's called a 'cue.' A cue is something that happens to let you know it's your turn to do something.

"For instance, when Humpty-Dumpty bounces off the ground and falls out of sight, Shauna knows it's time to bring up the cracked Humpty-Dumpty. And when the cracked Humpty-Dumpty appears, Evan and Kathy know it's time to bring in all the king's horses and all the king's men.

"We'll all try to remember our cues. But if one of us forgets, don't make a fuss, because the audience will hear. If there's a mistake or a missed cue, we'll quietly try to fix it. OK?"

■*Performance:* Yes, that's right . . . simple, short, and informal.

"Jack and Jill"

■*Production:* Cut out the figures and attach control rods. (See fig. 6.10.) The well can be taped to a half-circle of construction paper or half a paper doily.

■*Rehearsal:* After showing the scenery to the students, place it on the projector. Give the shadow figures to the first cast.

Before rehearsing, ask the students to try twisting the control rods so that the characters tumble head over heels when they fall. This move is exactly like the sinking ship in figure 4.9. It's easier to do if the puppets remain cutouts. The optional moving parts might make the tumble too hard for this age level (although the bending waists also make for good falls).

Have the characters approach the well from opposite sides of the screen so that puppeteers don't have to reach over each other. Check the preset. Lower the curtain.

"Tina, please enter Jill from the right side of the shadow screen. Charles, enter Jack from the left side. Climb the hill while we say the first part of the rhyme; then fall slowly down the hill during the second part. Here we go . . ."

Raise the curtain.

> *Jack and Jill went up the hill*
> *To fetch a pail of water.*
> *Jack fell down and broke his crown*
> *And Jill came tumbling after.*

Because this is a very short presentation with two characters, it's best to rehearse the first cast only once or twice before giving the next duo a turn. Succeeding players will learn their cues from watching the others.

■*Performance:* As usual.

Fig. 6.10.

STORIES

"The Three Billy Goats Gruff"

■*Production:* Cut out the figures and attach control rods. (See figs. 6.11 and 6.12, page 122.) The puppets might need extra-long sticks to reach the bridge midlevel on the shadow screen.

As mentioned earlier, incidental characters like birds and butterflies can be blended into a scene to provide additional roles. It's usually best to do this at the beginning or end of a scene so that the audience doesn't mistake these "walk-ons" (or "fly-ons") for major characters. Also, please don't use them when something dramatic or important occurs, as they can detract from the story.

Fig. 6.11.

Fig. 6.11 (continued)

Fig. 6.12.

The transparency scene can be a simple construction paper bridge connecting wax paper riverbanks with a separate sheet of wax paper for the undulating river. (See fig. 6.13.)

Fig. 6.13.

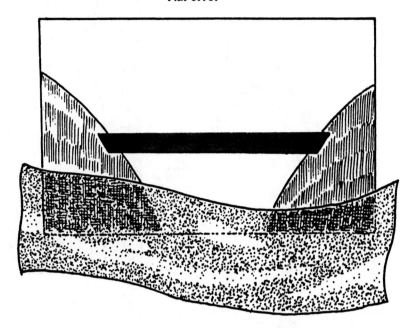

Of course, more elaborate settings are possible, as well as the following scene for copying to a transparency. (See fig. 6.14, page 124.)

This story can also incorporate a scene change, using the transparency from "Old MacDonald Had a Farm" (fig. 6.2) to open the show. Also, consider taping a piece of red Roscolux to the top of the reflecting lens so that it can be flipped down to color the entire scene.

So that students don't get confused about left and right when operating their puppets, stage directions are used for the first time. "Stage left" and "stage right" simply mean the performers' left and right as they face the audience. Because you'll also be on stage handling narration and scene changes, these stage directions also apply to your left and right. To prevent any confusion, draw a big L and R on 3"-x-5" cards and tack them to the sides of the shadow screen. (See fig. 6.15, page 125.)

■*Rehearsal:* Although this is a simple and repetitive story, it's more complicated than the previous songs and rhymes and is better suited for the older children of this age bracket. Practice the story and scene changes yourself until you're comfortable with them. That way, your entire attention can go to the rehearsal. (Also, please remember that the following narratives and stage directions are only suggestions. There's always more than one way to tell a story, and if you find better alternatives or simplifications, feel free to incorporate them.)

Fig. 6.14.

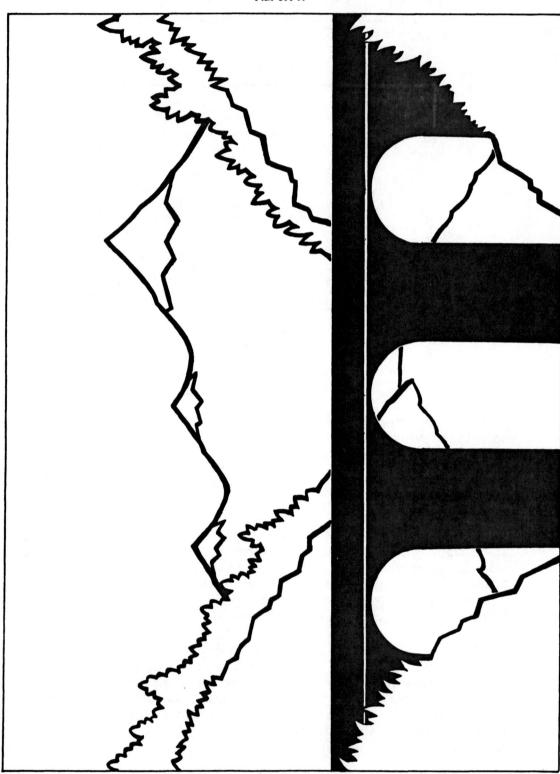

Please enlarge art 25% to fill an 8½-x-11" transparency from edge to edge.

From *Worlds of Shadow*. © 1996. Teacher Ideas Press. (800) 237-6124.

Fig. 6.15.

First, make sure that all the students are familiar with the story. Then, after showing the scenery to the students, place the farm scene on the projector. Distribute shadow puppets to the first cast.

Those operating the three goats should kneel behind the screen stage left in the characters' order of appearance: Baby Billy Goat Gruff, Mama Billy Goat Gruff, and Papa Billy Goat Gruff. The troll puppeteer should stay near the overhead projector. Any incidental birds and butterflies should enter and exit from stage right before the goats enter.

Check the preset. Bring down the curtain. Announce the title of the story. Raise the curtain.

The Three Billy Goats Gruff

Long ago, there lived a family of billy goats whose name was Gruff. There was Baby Billy Goat Gruff . . .

Baby Billy Goat Gruff crosses from stage left to stage right, turns around, and waits.

. . . and Mama Billy Goat Gruff . . .

Mama Billy Goat Gruff does the same.

. . . and Papa Billy Goat Gruff.

Papa Billy Goat Gruff crosses to the waiting family, facing them.

> *Papa Billy Goat Gruff said, "I have seen beautiful green pastures across the river. Let's cross over the bridge and graze there."*
> *"That sounds wonderful," said Mama and Baby Billy Goat Gruff.*

All three goats exit stage right. Raise up the farm scene and slowly slip down the piece of red Roscolux to color the entire screen.

> *But under the bridge lived a wicked ugly troll . . .*

Enter the troll to center stage on the overhead projector.

> *He was hungry all the time. His favorite food was . . . goat!*

As the troll exits, lower the bridge scene into focus and raise the red gel. The troll should move to the shadow screen and lurk under the bridge, stage left.

> *Baby Billy Goat Gruff was the first to cross the bridge. His little feet went "Trip, trap! Trip, trap! Trip, trap!" as he walked.*

Baby Billy Goat Gruff enters from stage right to the center of the bridge. The troll hops up and faces him.

> *"Who is walking across my bridge?" growled the troll.*
> *"It is I, Baby Billy Goat Gruff!"*
> *"I am going to eat you!" said the troll.*
> *"Do not eat me," said Baby Billy Goat Gruff. "I am small and skinny. If you let me cross, a much bigger goat will come along."*
> *"Very well," said the troll.*

The troll hops back down under the bridge. Baby Billy Goat Gruff crosses the bridge and exits stage left. Mama Billy Goat Gruff enters stage right.

> *Mama Billy Goat Gruff was next to cross the bridge. Her feet went "Trip! Trap! Trip! Trap! Trip! Trap!" as she walked.*

Mama Billy Goat Gruff crosses to the center of the bridge. The troll hops up and faces her.

> *"Who is walking across my bridge?" growled the troll.*
> *"It is I, Mama Billy Goat Gruff!"*
> *"I am going to eat you!" said the troll.*
> *"Do not eat me," said Mama Billy Goat Gruff. "I am small and skinny. If you let me cross, a much bigger goat will come along."*
> *"Very well," said the troll.*

The troll hops back down under the bridge. Mama Billy Goat Gruff crosses the bridge and exits stage left. Papa Billy Goat Gruff enters stage right.

Papa Billy Goat Gruff crossed the bridge. His feet went "TRIP! TRAP! TRIP! TRAP! TRIP! TRAP!" as he walked.

Papa Billy Goat Gruff crosses to the center of the bridge. The troll hops up and faces him.

"Who is walking across my bridge?" growled the troll.
"It is I, Papa Billy Goat Gruff!"
"I am going to eat you!" said the troll.
"I don't think so!" said Papa Billy Goat Gruff. He lowered his head and butted the wicked ugly troll into the river.

Direct one character to stay pressed against the screen and the other to remain slightly back to avoid torn puppets. (See fig. 4.10.) After getting butted, the troll falls off the bottom of the screen as Papa Billy Goat Gruff crosses the bridge and exits stage left. Incidental birds and butterflies can make another appearance as the curtain slowly descends and the narration ends.

The wicked ugly troll was never seen again. The Three Billy Goats Gruff enjoyed grazing in the green meadow forever after. The end.

Practice this story in sections if the students have trouble remembering their placement and movements. Review previous "blocking" (the theater term for stage movement) before tackling a new segment.

■*Performance:* With a full-fledged story, it would be nice to have a perfect performance. But even when everybody is well rehearsed and attentive, things sometimes go wrong. Backward puppets make late entrances, control rods come loose, puppeteers fall over. (And I'm talking about our shows!) So please don't get overly concerned about "perfect" performances at this or any other age level. Besides, most students are striving to do their best and are often their own severest critics.

Other than remaining calm, the most helpful thing to do is to keep a roll of masking tape around your wrist for emergency control rod repair.

"The Three Little Pigs"

■*Production:* This longer story is markedly similar in structure to the previous one yet provides a few new techniques. After cutting out the figures and attaching control rods (figs. 6.16 and 6.17, page 130), cut out the houses of the three little pigs (fig. 6.18, page 131). Add a stick-controlled door to each if you like. If you'd like to add color to the houses, tape part of a transparency to the back of each and tint it with marker pens or transparent Form-X film.

(Text continues on page 132.)

Fig. 6.16.

Fig. 6.17.

Fig. 6.18.

From *Worlds of Shadow*. © 1996. Teacher Ideas Press. (800) 237-6124.

A title transparency makes a nice introduction to this tale, though it really requires only a forest scene. This can be made of strips of construction paper on wax paper or green transparent Form-X film ground. (See fig. 6.19.)

Fig. 6.19.

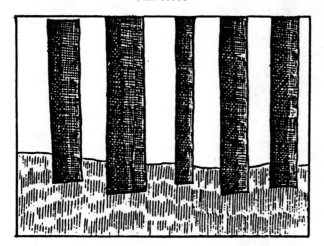

As before, a scene is offered for copying and coloring. (See fig. 6.20.)

You'll also need to cut out the cooking pot and have a red gel handy for the flame (just like the rocket ship blastoff effect described in Chapter 5).

■*Rehearsal:* Again, this is a simple and familiar story that's more complex than the preceding songs and rhymes, making it more suitable for the older children of this age level. Once more, it's a good idea to practice the story and scene changes before rehearsal.

You can also decide how grim you'd like this Grimm tale to be. Although it's "kinder and gentler" for the first two pigs to run away from the wolf and hide in their wise brother's house, the resulting crowd behind the shadow screen can be a problem. If this confluence of puppets and bodies becomes a tangle, the pigs should be eaten by the wolf or hide in the forest until the story's end. Either way, fewer characters make for an easier rehearsal.

After making sure that all the students know the story, show the scenery to them. Place the reversed title transparency on the projector. Distribute shadow puppets to the first cast.

Fig. 6.20.

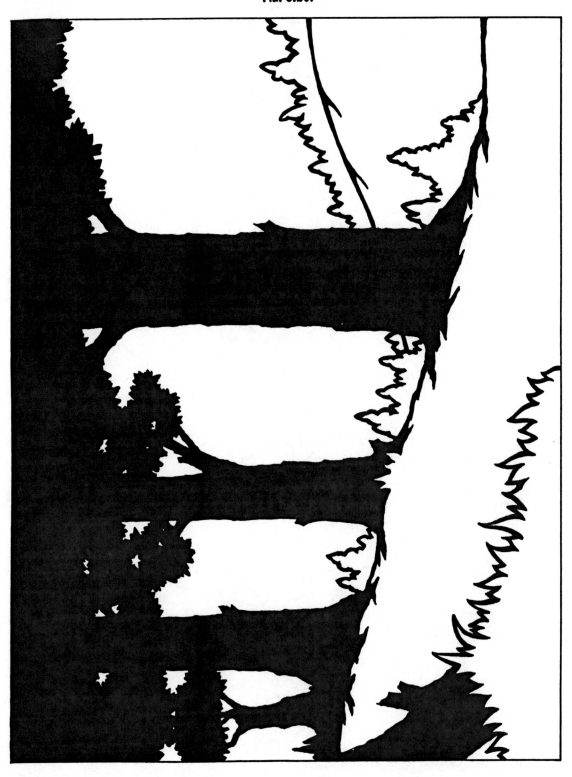

Please enlarge art 25% to fill an 8½-x-11" transparency from edge to edge.

Have the students operating the three little pigs stand near the stage-left side of the overhead projector. Check the preset. Lower the curtain; then raise it to reveal the title.

The Three Little Pigs

Raise the title card up and out as the three little pigs slowly cross the projection stage one at a time from stage left to stage right.

> *Once upon a time in a land far away, there lived three little pigs.*
> *The first little pig was quite lazy . . .*
> *The second little pig was lazier still . . .*
> *But the third little pig was different. He worked very hard.*

After the third little pig exits, have the puppeteers kneel stage right at the shadow screen. Get ready to enter the first little pig's house of straw from the bottom center of the projection stage.

The first little pig enters and stops at midscreen, moving his arm to build the straw house. Ease in the house from the bottom of the projection stage.

> *The first little pig quickly built a house of straw. Then he ran out to play.*

As the first little pig exits stage left, lift up the straw house to make a scene change. When the second little pig enters stage right and crosses to midscreen, slowly slide in the house of sticks as he moves his arm to build it.

> *The second little pig quickly made a flimsy house of sticks. Then he ran out to play.*

As the second little pig exits stage left, lift up the stick house. As the third little pig enters stage right and crosses to midscreen, move in the house of bricks for him to construct.

> *But the third little pig thought long and hard about his house. He decided to make it out of brick. It took a long time to build. It was very hard work.*

The first two pigs enter stage left and look at their industrious kin. The house appears only halfway.

> *The other little pigs thought their brother was silly. "Why work so hard when you can play?" they said.*
> *"You'll find out when the big bad wolf comes to your door!" said the third little pig.*

The first two pigs exit stage left. The third little pig continues working until the house appears completely.

> *Finally, the third little pig finished his house of bricks. "There!" he said. "Now it's time to play."*

The third little pig exits stage left as his brick house is lifted up for a scene change to the forest. The wolf enters stage right, prowls through the trees, and exits stage left. Then have the wolf slowly cross the projection stage in close-up, also from stage right to stage left. When he finishes his appearance, have the wolf puppeteer kneel stage left.

> *In the deep dark forest, the big bad wolf was hungry. Very hungry! He came out of the forest and saw the three little pigs outside their houses. "Yum, yum!" he said.*

Make a scene change from the forest scene to the house of straw, which should project stage right on the shadow screen. The first little pig runs in from stage left and enters the house. The wolf enters stage left and crosses to the house.

> *The first little pig saw the wolf and ran into his house of straw.*
> *"Little pig! Little pig! Let me in!" said the wolf.*
> *"Not by the hair of my chinny-chin-chin!" said the first little pig.*
> *"Then I'll huff and I'll puff and I'll blow your house in!" said the wolf.*
> *And he did just that!*

As the wolf blows, move the straw house off the projector stage right, leaving the first little pig exposed. If he runs away, have him exit stage right. If he gets eaten, have him go off the bottom of the shadow screen as the wolf bends over him.

> *The first little pig got gobbled up (or "ran away and hid in the forest!"). Then the wolf chased after the second little pig.*

After the wolf exits stage left, bring the stick house down into focus so that it projects stage right on the shadow screen. When the second little pig runs into it from stage left, have the wolf enter from stage left again.

> *The second little pig saw the wolf and ran into his house of sticks.*
> *"Little pig! Little pig! Let me in!" said the wolf.*
> *"Not by the hair of my chinny-chin-chin!" said the second little pig.*
> *"Then I'll huff and I'll puff and I'll blow your house in!" said the wolf.*
> *And he did just that!*

Again, move the stick house off stage right as the wolf huffs and puffs. The second little pig is now in harm's way.

> *The second little pig got gobbled up (or "ran away and hid in the forest!"). Then the wolf chased after the third little pig.*

After the second little pig gets eaten or runs away stage right, bring the brick house down into focus after the wolf's exit stage left. Again, the house should project on the stage-right side of the shadow screen. When the third little pig runs into it from stage left, have the wolf enter from stage left again.

The third little pig saw the wolf and ran into his house of bricks.
"Little pig! Little pig! Let me in!" said the wolf.
"Not by the hair of my chinny-chin-chin!" said the third little pig.
"Then I'll huff and I'll puff and I'll blow your house in!" said the wolf.
"Be my guest," said the third little pig.
The wolf huffed and puffed, but he couldn't blow that house in! It was too strong.

Wobble the brick house just a tiny bit to show the wolf's huffing and puffing.

"I know what I'll do," said the wolf. "I'll sneak in through the chimney!"

Move the house down on the projection stage so that the wolf can jump on top of the roof. (The third little pig will have to move down with it.) Then lower the cooking pot into focus as the house goes off the projection stage and all characters exit the bottom of the shadow screen. Flicker the red gel in front of the projector's reflecting lens.

Have the wolf puppeteer come over to the overhead projector.

But the third little pig was ready! He had a big pot of hot water boiling over the fire. When the wolf came down the chimney . . . YEEEOWWWW! He landed right in the pot!

Move the wolf down the projection stage into the cooking pot. Again, the level of carnage is your choice. The wolf can disappear into the pot and get cooked, or scald himself and jump back up the chimney. Either way . . .

The big bad wolf was never seen again.

Lift up the cooking pot and bring the title transparency down into focus. Have the third little pig (or all three little pigs) do a final cross on the projection stage from stage right to stage left.

And the third little pig (or "three little pigs") lived happily ever after. The end.

Bring down the curtain.

If you divide this longer story into short segments for less tiring rehearsals, always review what was blocked previously.

■*Performance:* Keep that roll of masking tape on your wrist.

Congratulations! You have successfully steered a group of preschoolers through the production, rehearsal, and performance of a shadow puppet show. This also makes you capable of governing a large midwestern state. If that doesn't sound challenging, go on to the productions in Chapter 7.

Production, Rehearsal, and Performance with Ages Six to Seven

Shadow puppetry with this age level doesn't differ greatly in method or complexity from that with younger children. Because drawing and cutting skills are still developing, teachers and aides will again need to assist students with puppets and projected scenery. And although first- and second-graders might trumpet individual maturity, group cooperation can be questionable. So presentations should remain simple, straightforward, and relatively brief.

This chapter is mainly an extension of Chapter 6, containing directions and techniques for dramatizing familiar stories. This age level might dismiss simple songs and nursery rhymes as kid stuff, but stories (especially these age-old standards) are usually still embraced. In fact, "The Three Billy Goats Gruff" and "The Three Little Pigs" remain excellent introductory productions for this age group. Here are a few more.

"Little Red Riding Hood"

■*Production:* In addition to the characters in figures 7.1, page 138, and 7.2, page 139, use the wolf in figure 6.16 from "The Three Little Pigs." The figures of Red Riding Hood, the wolf and the wolf-in-disguise have one moving part; Grandma and the woodcutter have the option of two. Please use the configuration you feel most comfortable with (including no moving parts). Cut out the characters and attach control rods. (A control rod on Grandma's hand doubles as a walking stick.)

This story can also display a number of incidental characters when scenes are introduced or just ending. Barnyard animals in the farm scene will work well, as will butterflies, birds, and woodland creatures in the forest scene.

Besides the farm scene from "Old MacDonald Had a Farm" (fig. 6.2) and the forest scene from "The Three Little Pigs" (fig. 6.20), you'll also need transparencies for outside and inside Grandma's house. These can be made from scratch or copied and colored from figures 7.3 (page 140) and 7.4 (page 141). A title card is again optional.

(Text continues on page 142.)

Fig. 7.1.

Fig. 7.2.

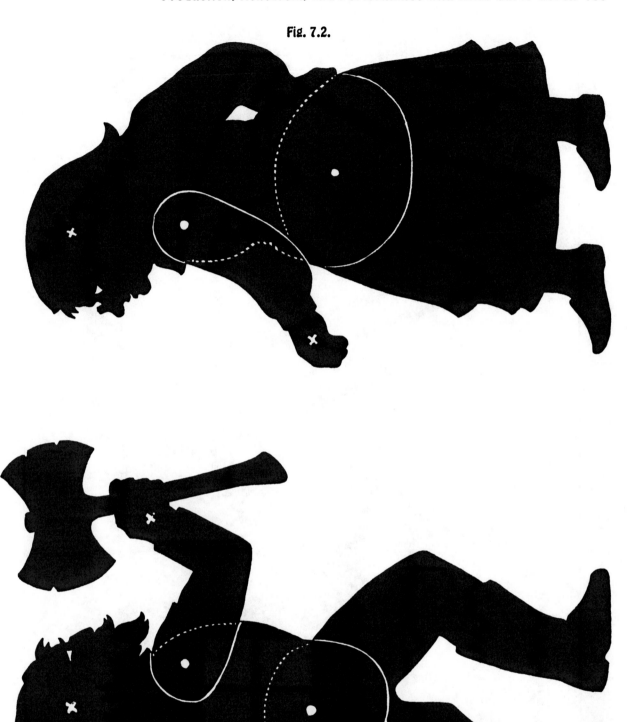

From *Worlds of Shadow*. © 1996. Teacher Ideas Press. (800) 237-6124.

Fig. 7.3.

Please enlarge art 25% to fill an 8½-x-11" transparency from edge to edge.

From *Worlds of Shadow.* © 1996. Teacher Ideas Press. (800) 237-6124.

Fig. 7.4.

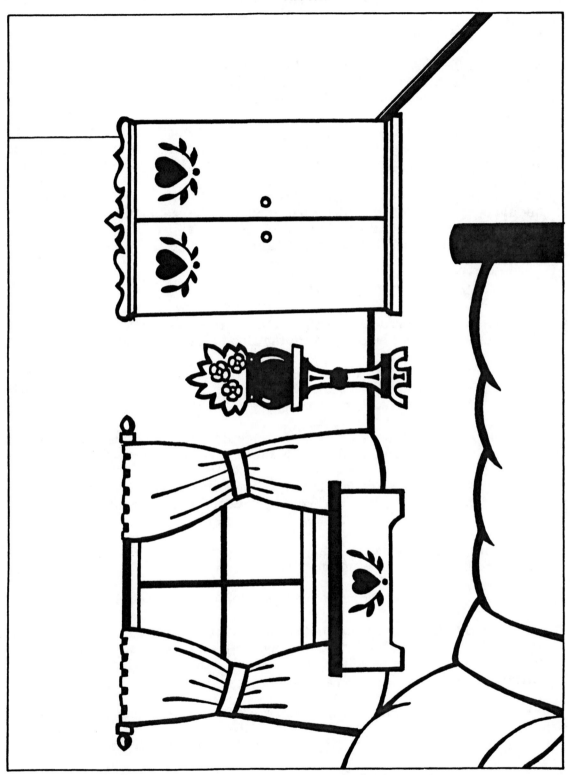

Please enlarge art 25% to fill an 8½-x-11" transparency from edge to edge.

From *Worlds of Shadow.* © 1996. Teacher Ideas Press. (800) 237-6124.

For this tale you can also use student shadows against the screen for the first scene. Please select two girls and have them wear headscarves to play Red Riding Hood and her mother.

■*Rehearsal:* After practicing the story and scene changes before rehearsal, acquaint the students with the tale. Then demonstrate the scenery and distribute shadow puppets to the first cast.

Have the girl in headscarf playing Red Riding Hood stand offscreen stage left; the headscarfed girl playing Mother stands offscreen with a picnic basket stage right. The puppeteer operating Red Riding Hood should be kneeling stage left.

Place the optional title card in reverse on the projector. The other scenes should be in the following order: farm scene, forest scene, outside Grandma's house, and inside Grandma's house.

Check the preset. Lower the curtain. Announce the title and raise the curtain.

Little Red Riding Hood

Raise the title card and change to the farm scene. Incidental characters should enter and exit before Red Riding Hood and Mother enter.

> *Once upon a time there was a little girl named Red Riding Hood. That was not her real name, of course. She was called that because of the bright red hood and cape she always wore.*

Both girls with headscarves enter to center screen and face each other. Mother hands the picnic basket to Red Riding Hood, who curtsies.

> *One day, Red Riding Hood's mother called to her. "Grandma isn't feeling well," she said. "Would you take this basket of goodies to her?" "Certainly," said Little Red Riding Hood.*

Both girls turn and exit. The puppeteer operating Red Riding Hood enters the figure stage left, crossing the screen.

> *Little Red Riding Hood began the journey to Grandma's house.*

As Red Riding Hood exits stage right, change scenes from farm to forest. The wolf puppeteer should kneel stage left and get ready to enter. Any incidental characters should enter now and exit before Red Riding Hood's entrance.

> *She had to pass the deep dark forest where wild animals lived.*

Red Riding Hood enters stage right and crosses to center screen.

> *Wild animals like . . . the wolf!*

The wolf enters stage left and faces Red Riding Hood.

> *"What's in the basket, Little Red Riding Hood?" asked the wolf.*
> *"Goodies for my Grandma," said Little Red Riding Hood. "They are not for you!"*
> *"We shall see!" growled the wolf. Then he ran away.*

The wolf turns and exits stage left. Red Riding Hood also exits stage left, but more slowly. As she leaves, change scenes from forest to outside Grandma's house (with the house on the stage-right side of the shadow screen). Have the Grandma puppeteer kneel stage right and be ready to enter. The wolf enters stage left and crosses to the house. When he knocks on the door, Grandma enters so that she can be seen in the window.

> *The wolf took a shortcut to Grandma's house and got there before Little Red Riding Hood. He knocked at the door.*
> *"Who is knocking at my door?" asked Grandma.*
> *"It is Little Red Riding Hood," squeaked the wolf, changing his voice. "I have a basket of goodies for you."*
> *"Delightful!" said Grandma. "Come in, dear!"*

The wolf enters the house and Grandma screams. At this point, you need to make a decision about how to dispose of Grandma, if only temporarily. In the original, she was eaten, but she can just as effectively be locked in a closet or chased into the woods. Regardless of choice, have both characters exit stage right. Then, if Grandma runs away, have her reenter from stage right, cross the screen, and exit stage left.

Have the wolf-in-disguise puppeteer stand near the overhead projector.

> *The wolf gobbled up Grandma ("locked Grandma in the closet," "chased Grandma into the woods"), then disguised himself in her clothes.*

As you lift the scene, have the wolf-in-disguise cross the projector in close-up. As the character exits, lower the scene inside Grandma's house (with the bed on the stage-right side of the shadow screen). Have the wolf-in-disguise puppeteer kneel stage right; then enter the character.

> *It wasn't long before Little Red Riding Hood came along and knocked at the door.*
> *"Who is knocking at my door?" asked the wolf in his squeaky voice.*
> *"It is Little Red Riding Hood," said Little Red Riding Hood. "I have a basket of goodies for you."*
> *"Delightful!" said the wolf. "Come in, dear!"*

Red Riding Hood enters stage left and crosses to the disguised wolf.

> *"Why, Grandma!" said Little Red Riding Hood. "What big eyes you have!"*
> *"All the better to see you with," said the wolf.*

"And Grandma!" said Little Red Riding Hood. "What big ears you have!"

"All the better to hear you with," said the wolf.

"And Grandma!" said Little Red Riding Hood. "What big teeth you have!"

"All the better to eat you with!" growled the wolf. He leaped out of bed and chased after Little Red Riding Hood.

Red Riding Hood turns and exits stage left with the wolf close behind. Red Riding Hood reenters from stage left, followed again by the wolf.

This simple direction is a bit more involved than it sounds because the puppets must "cross over." Once the Red Riding Hood figure reenters, the puppeteer operating the wolf-in-disguise must bring his puppet and body back for the other puppeteer to cross in front. (See fig. 7.5.) Although this crossover happens offstage, some practice might be necessary to prevent a tangle.

Fig. 7.5.

As both characters exit stage right, move the scene up and out. Then have them come up to the projector and cross it in close-up. Bring down the scene outside Grandma's house as the puppeteers return to kneeling stage right. Once it's in focus, have Red Riding Hood enter stage right, cross the screen, and exit stage left. Have the woodcutter puppeteer ready to enter stage left.

But a brave woodcutter heard Little Red Riding Hood's cries for help. He ran to her rescue.

"Uh-oh!" said the wolf.

The woodcutter enters stage left as the wolf enters stage right. The wolf stops, then turns and runs back into the house stage right. The woodcutter goes after him, both exiting stage right. Then the wolf reenters (another crossover!), followed again by the woodcutter. After both characters exit stage left, have them cross in close-up on the projector.

The woodcutter chased the wolf away. He was never seen again.

The woodcutter and Little Red Riding Hood enter stage left. (If Grandma was locked in the closet, have her enter stage right from the house. If she was chased into the woods, have her enter stage left. If gobbled up . . . oh, well.)

Bring down the curtain as the narration finishes.

Everyone lived happily ever after. The end.

Consider dividing the rehearsal into segments to avoid wearing out performers or giving them too much to memorize. Review previous blocking when rehearsal begins anew. As noted earlier, extra practice might be necessary for smooth crossovers.

Also, caution performers to stay low even after their shadow puppets exit a scene. Many times a puppet's exit is followed immediately by the enormous shadow of a standing puppeteer who forgot his body would block the scene!

Above all, take your time and be patient. This is especially true if you elect to use the close-up chases on the overhead projector. It'll take a moment or two for the students to get back and forth from the screen. Just make scene changes slower to accommodate their travel time.

■*Performance:* As usual, please keep a performance as close to a rehearsal as possible: very informal and uncritical. Keep it fun.

Should there be any grousing about a tale being babyish (a rare but not unheard of attitude at this age), announce that the show will be performed for kindergartners. This shifts attention from the content of the story to its presentation and acceptance by a younger audience. This transfer of focus has even allowed world-weary fifth-graders to enthusiastically present "Little Red Riding Hood."

However, this declaration can make some students too aware that a performance is scheduled, engendering stage fright. The best remedy for "butterflies in the stomach" is the maintenance of a low-key attitude toward the production. In addition, assure the children that feeling nervous before a show is perfectly normal and that professional actors feel it, too.

"Goldilocks and the Three Bears"

■*Production:* After cutting out and attaching control rods to the shadow puppets (figs. 7.6 and 7.7, page 148), make transparency interior scenes of the three bears' kitchen, living room and bedroom, using the art in figures 7.8, page 149, 7.9, page 150, and 7.10, page 151 if you wish. Then cut out Baby Bear's chair and attach it to the living room scene with a paper fastener so that it can tilt when broken by Goldilocks.

The exterior scene of Grandma's house from "Little Red Riding Hood" (fig. 7.3) and the forest scene from "The Three Little Pigs" (fig. 6.20) will also be necessary. A title card is optional, as are incidental characters.

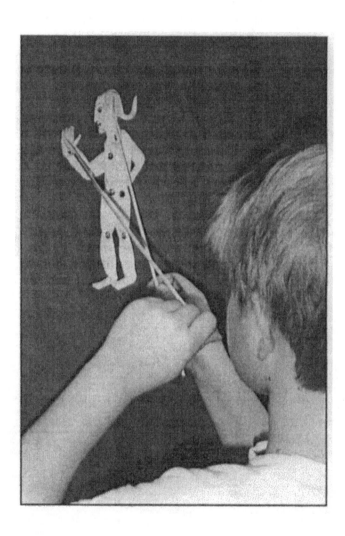

(Text continues on page 152.)

Fig. 7.6.

Fig. 7.7.

Fig. 7.8.

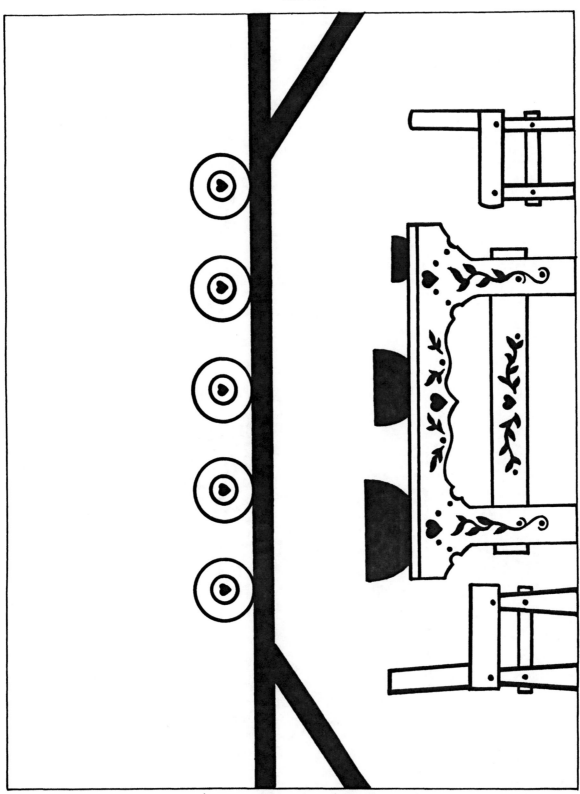

Please enlarge art 25% to fill an 8½-x-11" transparency from edge to edge.

Fig. 7.9.

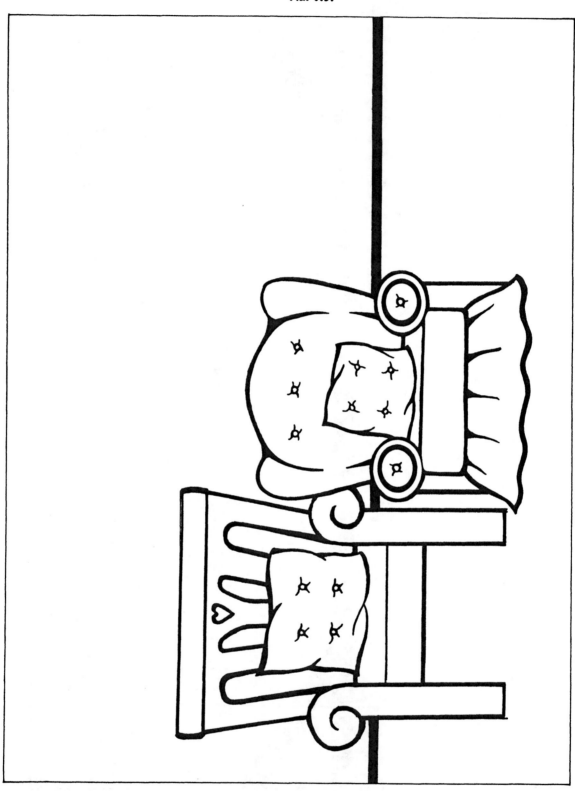

Please enlarge art 25% to fill an 8½-x-11" transparency from edge to edge.

From *Worlds of Shadow.* © 1996. Teacher Ideas Press. (800) 237-6124.

Fig. 7.10.

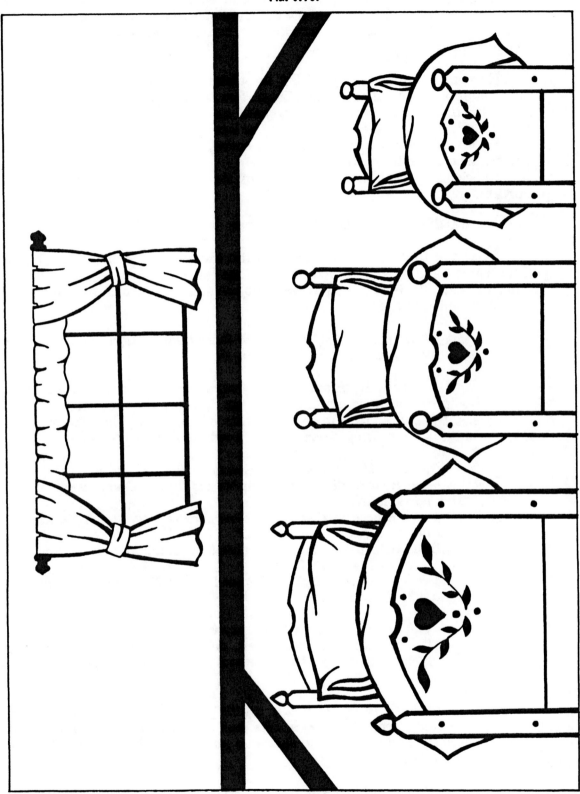

Please enlarge art 25% to fill an 8½-x-11" transparency from edge to edge.

■*Rehearsal:* Again, rehearse the tale and scene changes yourself before including the students. Then show the transparency scenes and appoint the first cast. (As Goldilocks is onscreen a lot, consider sharing the role between two or three people.)

Have the puppeteers operating the three bears kneeling stage right in order of appearance: Papa Bear, Mama Bear, and Baby Bear.

With the optional title card reversed on the projector, stack the other scenes in the following order: outside the bears' house, kitchen scene, living room scene, bedroom scene, and forest scene. Some of these transparencies will be used more than once.

Check the preset. Lower the curtain. Announce the title and raise the curtain.

Goldilocks and the Three Bears

Raise the title card and change to the scene outside the bears' house. (The house should be projected on the stage-left side of the shadow screen.) Once in focus, the bears enter stage right one at a time, cross the screen, and exit stage left into the house.

> *Once upon a time, there were three bears. There was Papa Bear . . . and Mama Bear . . . and Baby Bear.*

Change the scene from outside the bears' house to the kitchen. (Papa Bear's big porridge bowl should be stage left on the screen.) To avoid crossovers, the bears enter in reverse order of their exit: Baby Bear, Mama Bear, and Papa Bear. They cross to their bowls of porridge.

> *One day, Mama Bear made porridge for breakfast.*
> *Papa Bear tasted some from his big bowl. "Goodness!" he said. "This porridge is too hot!"*
> *Mama Bear tasted some from her middle-sized bowl. "Goodness!" she said. "It is rather hot, isn't it?"*
> *Baby Bear tasted some from his little bowl. "Yow!" he said. "Too hot!"*
> *"Let's go for a walk," said Papa Bear. "When we come back, the porridge will be just right."*

The bears exit stage left. Change scenes from the kitchen to outside the bears' house. The bears reenter stage left, cross the screen, and exit stage right. The Goldilocks puppeteer should kneel stage right and enter her after the bears leave.

> *After the three bears left, a little girl wandered out of the forest. Her name was Goldilocks. She had gotten lost and was tired and hungry. She smelled the delicious porridge and went into the three bears' house.*

After entering, Goldilocks pauses at center screen, then exits into the house stage left. Change scenes from outside the bears' house to the kitchen.

Goldilocks tasted the porridge from Papa Bear's big bowl. It was too hot.
Then she tasted some from Mama Bear's middle-sized bowl. It was too cold.
Goldilocks tasted some from Baby Bear's little bowl. It was just right. She ate it all up.

Goldilocks exits stage right. Change scenes from the kitchen to the living room with three chairs. (Papa Bear's big chair should be stage right on the screen.) Goldilocks reenters stage right and goes from chair to chair. Tilt Baby Bear's chair when it breaks.

Goldilocks wanted to sit down and rest.
She tried Papa Bear's big chair, but it was too hard.
She tried Mama Bear's middle-sized chair, but it was too soft.
She tried Baby Bear's little chair. It was just right. But it broke.
Now Goldilocks wanted to lie down and sleep.

As Goldilocks exits stage left, change scenes from the living room to the bedroom. (Papa Bear's big bed should be stage left on the screen.) Goldilocks reenters stage left and tries each bed.

She tried Papa Bear's big bed, but it was too hard.
She tried Mama Bear's middle-sized bed, but it was too soft.
She tried Baby Bear's little bed. It was just right. Goldilocks fell fast asleep.

Change scenes from the bedroom to the forest. The three bears enter stage right with Papa Bear first.

The three bears had gone for a very long walk.
"I think the porridge will be just right now," said Papa Bear. "Let's go home."

The bears turn and exit stage right. Change scenes from the forest to the kitchen. The bears reenter stage right with Papa Bear again in the lead. They go to their bowls.

When the three bears got home, they noticed something was wrong.
"Someone's been eating my porridge," said Papa Bear.
"Someone's been eating my porridge," said Mama Bear.
"Someone's been eating my porridge," said Baby Bear. "And they ate it all up!"

The three bears exit stage left as the scene changes from the kitchen to the living room. The bears reenter stage left and go to their chairs.

> *"Someone's been sitting in my chair," said Papa Bear.*
> *"Someone's been sitting in my chair," said Mama Bear.*
> *"Someone's been sitting in my chair," said Baby Bear. "And they broke it all to pieces!"*

The three bears exit stage left as the scene changes from the living room to the bedroom. Goldilocks reenters stage right on Baby Bear's bed.

> *"Someone's been sleeping in my bed," said Papa Bear.*
> *"Someone's been sleeping in my bed," said Mama Bear.*
> *"Someone's been sleeping in my bed," said Baby Bear. "And she still is!"*
> *At that moment, Goldilocks woke up and saw the three bears. She screamed and ran away home.*

Goldilocks exits stage right. Bring down the curtain as the narration ends.

> *"What a frightening visitor!" said Papa Bear.*
> *"Perhaps we should lock the door the next time we go out," said Mama Bear.*
> *"Let's eat breakfast!" said Baby Bear.*
> *The end.*

This story has a lot of scene changes and character movement, but at least everybody enters and reenters without crossovers or crawling from one side of the screen to the other. As noted earlier, the role of Goldilocks should probably be a collective one.

■*Performance:* Altogether now: "Brief! Informal! Uncritical!"

Up to this point, the teacher has been the mainstay of presentations, providing puppet patterns and transparency art for production, as well as stage directions, narration, and scene changes for rehearsal and performance. In the productions for ages eight through twelve that are covered in Chapter 10, students begin to shoulder some of these responsibilities. But first, let's take a look at some intermediate shadow puppet and projected scenery techniques that older performers can incorporate into their epics.

8

Intermediate Shadow Puppet Techniques for Ages Eight to Twelve

This is a wide age range, but there are seldom clearly defined boundaries as to what's appropriate for a specific group of children. Some of the previous productions might work with fifth-graders, and parts of these intermediate chapters could be used with second-graders. Only the teacher knows for sure. So pick what you find applicable from the following methods of construction, operation, and alternative shadow figures. They aren't difficult and can add a great deal to a production.

CONSTRUCTION

Although poster paper and brass paper fasteners remain the basics of shadow puppet construction, there are methods and materials suitable for older students that produce more finished and versatile figures.

Cutting with Craft (X-Acto) Knives

Up to this point, students have probably cut out shadow puppets with blunt scissors and the help of a teacher or aide. Now, this level's younger students can use real scissors without a medical team standing by. And older children can graduate to an X-Acto knife *if* properly trained and supervised. This news might send chills down your spine, but it really is the best instrument for elaborate exterior cuts and interior details.

First, find out if these extremely sharp craft knives (fig. 8.1, page 156) are even allowed in your school. (In some urban areas, they're classified as weapons and even art teachers can't use them.)

Fig. 8.1.

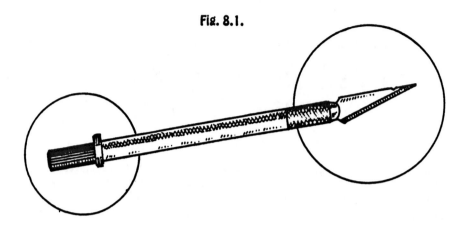

1. *Knife choices:* Choose a nonswiveling knife with a #11 blade, safety cap, and a rear blade release. (The latter keeps student fingers at the back of the knife when loosening and tightening the blade collar.) X-Acto manufactures two likely candidates, both available from art and craft stores:

    a. X-Acto X-Press Rear Release Knife (Mfg. #3699): This basic 5" aluminum knife with safety cap and rear release costs about $5.

    b. X-Acto Gripster Knife (Mfg. #3628): This knife has not only a safety cap and rear release but also a hexagonal handle nut to prevent rolling and a soft rubberized barrel for better grip. It comes in five colors and it's a dollar cheaper!

2. *Replacement blades:* X-Acto #11 blades can be purchased in packs of 5 (Mfg. #211 at about $2 each), safety dispenser packs of 15 (Mfg. #411 at almost $5 each), and economical bulk packs of 100 (Mfg. #611 ranging from $20 to $24).

3. *Cutting surfaces:* Although heavy cardboard prevents tabletop damage, it dulls knives quickly and soon falls apart with repeated use. Masking-taped window glass is better, but its unyielding surface causes blades to skid. The best solution is a self-sealing cutting mat. Available at art and craft outlets and office supply stores, these rectangles of rubberized plastic can absorb years of puppet making and still maintain a smooth surface. Manufactured in translucent white and a less expensive green, they range in size from 9" x 12" (about $12) to 24" x 36" (about $60).

4. *Cutting hints:* After cautioning students about the blade's very sharp edge, show how to cut with it. (See fig. 8.2.) Holding the knife like a pencil, anchor the poster paper with your other hand. Then bear down and cut using the point and top edge of the blade. (Initially, quite a few students hold the knife perpendicular to the poster paper and scrape away with the point alone.) If an angle is awkward, approach it from another direction rather than cutting from an uncomfortable or dangerous hand position.

Fig. 8.2.

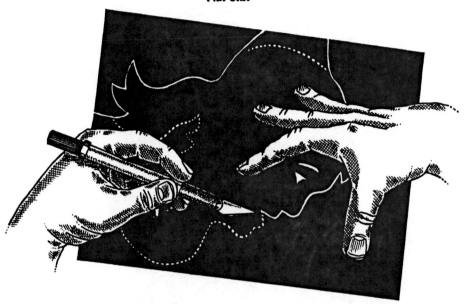

Fully Jointed Shadow Puppets

"How many sticks can I put on my puppet?" ask workshop students.

"As many as you have hands for," we reply.

Two control rods are usually all that are necessary to operate most characters. Of course, there are exceptions to every rule. Overhead views of birds, bats, butterflies, and spiders constitute one. (See fig. 8.3, page 158.)

Fig. 8.3.

Another is when a genuinely complex figure demands operation by more than one puppeteer. (See fig. 8.4.) Otherwise, additional rods often make figures look like they've hung around the wrong end of a javelin practice.

Fig. 8.4.

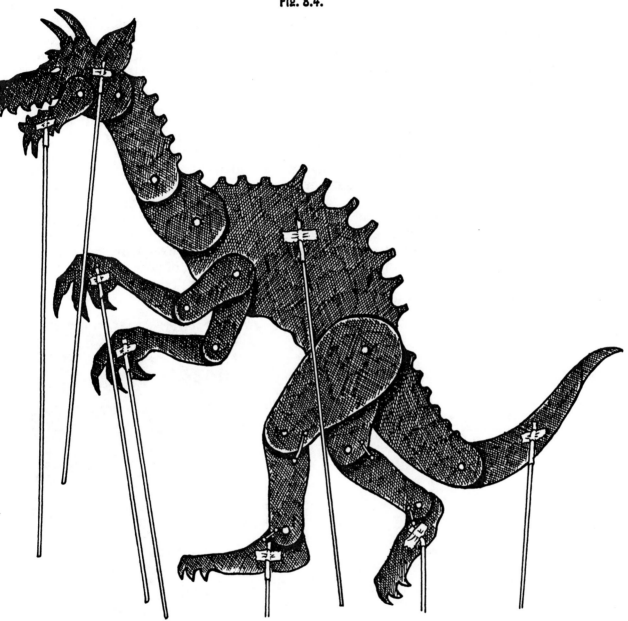

The following pages indicate a number of ways to joint fully articulated figures with a minimum of control rods. As before, circles indicate holes for brass paper fasteners and Xs indicate the approximate attachment of control rods. Also, a solid white line means a section overlaps the portion marked with a dotted line.

Figure 8.5 shows a variety of joints for four-legged animals. The boy and girl in figure 8.6 (page 162) need to stand on the frame of the shadow screen to provide resistance for hip and knee movement. It's worthwhile to sew or glue a short length of string or yarn behind each knee to prevent the leg from swinging in the wrong direction. This measure is crucial if ankle joints are added to the figures. Otherwise, the feet will hang straight down.

The shark of figure 8.7 (page 163) illustrates the moving mouth and tail common to many sea creatures; the squid gives another example of the one-handed operation of two parts sharing a common pivot point (as in figure 8.3).

Figure 8.8 (page 164) contains a number of ideas that can be adapted to other figures. The turtle sports a sliding neck and a simple set of swinging rear legs given added weight with a taped-on penny. The cobra can sway gently up and down but would require practice for a quick strike. The inchworm could get away with two control sticks unless the middle collapses, in which case a third one is necessary to pop it back up. The kangaroo demonstrates a leg joint that can also be used for rabbits and raptors, as well as the inclusion of both arms in a single section. The elephant's trunk is easy to operate but requires precise jointing and trimming to look natural.

(Text continues on page 165.)

Fig. 8.5.

Fig. 8.6.

Fig. 8.7.

Fig. 8.8.

Control Rod Alternatives

For those who have outgrown drinking straws and fondue sticks, we suggest umbrella rods for shadow puppets operated against the screen. (See fig. 8.9.) These can be clipped out of discarded or secondhand full-sized umbrellas with a pair of tin snips. (The collapsible purse variety won't work, though, because the rods are too short.)

Besides the obvious advantage of length, umbrella rods are worthwhile because of the eyelets at their ends. Designed for attaching umbrella fabric, they make excellent openings for connecting shadow puppets.

First, poke a hole through the figure with a beaded dressmaker's pin. Then bend the pin in a right angle close to the bead with a small pair of pliers. Stick the pin through the umbrella rod and the figure, then use masking tape to secure the pin on the opposite side. (Of course, these rods can also be fastened with the masking tape tabs used previously.)

Once on the projector, however, all control rods look thick and unwieldy. A less visible alternative is .0075 or .010 millimeter clear acetate, available in 30"-x-40" sheets from art supply stores. Thin strips of this sturdy transparent plastic can be taped to the moving parts of overhead projector puppets much like opaque control rods. (See fig. 8.10, page 166.) Because the acetate is flexible, tape tabs are not absolutely necessary. In fact, these strips sometimes work better when operated absolutely flat. (Because flat movement limits side-to-side flexibility, the strip's angle of attachment to the figure may need adjustment.)

Fig. 8.9.

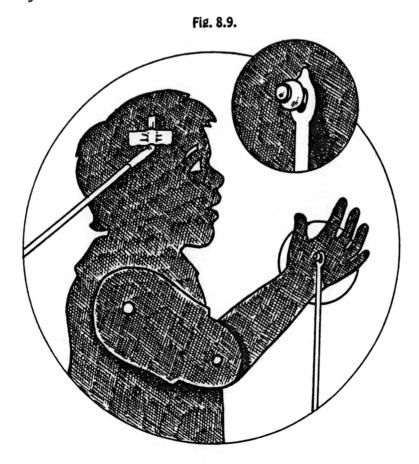

Without the rigidity of control rods, some practice will be necessary to achieve accurate movements. Make sure that figures with acetate strips are stored flat to prevent bends and creases.

Fig. 8.10.

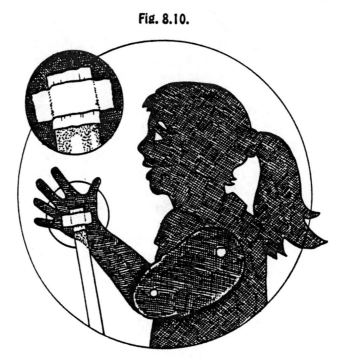

OPERATION

Transforming Shadow Puppets

In many folktales and fairy stories, characters grow, shrink, or turn into completely different creatures. All these transformations are possible with the overhead projector. The process is much like changing transparency scenes. Four variations follow and are charted in figure 8.11.

1. *Screen-to-screen transformation:* Pull the first character back from the screen toward the reflecting lens of the projector. Its shadow will grow increasingly large and indistinct. When the first character is almost to the lens, place the second figure in front of it. Move out the first character; then bring the second figure up to the screen.

    For this transformation to work properly, the shadow puppets must stay in a direct line back and forth from the reflecting lens.

2. *Screen-to-stage transformation:* As before, pull the first character back from the screen toward the reflecting lens. When it's almost to the lens, place the second figure underneath the reflecting lens. Move out the first character; then lower the second figure to the projection stage.

    If the first character is just getting bigger, use the same figure throughout. After bringing it to the front of the lens, quickly slip it underneath and then lower it.

Fig. 8.11.

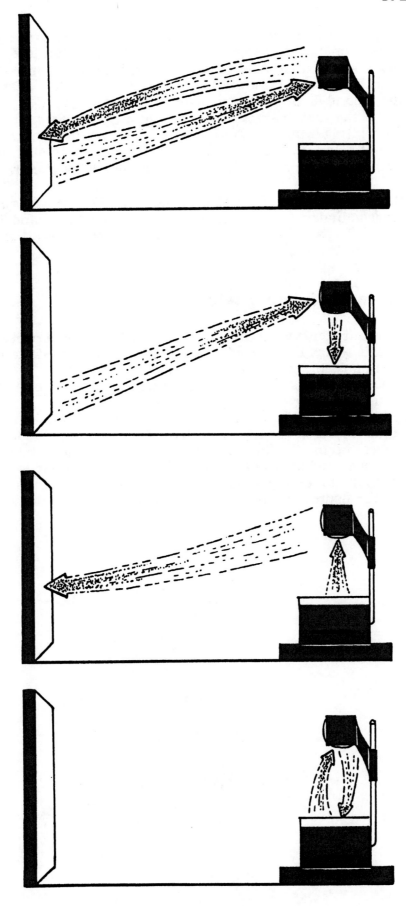

3. *Stage-to-screen transformation:* This process is essentially the reverse of Screen-to-stage transformation. Raise the first character from the projection stage to underneath the reflecting lens. When it is in place, put the second figure in front of the lens. Remove the first character and bring the second figure up to the shadow screen.

   If the first character is shrinking, use the same figure throughout. After lifting it underneath the lens, slide it in front of the lens and move it to the screen. Again, the shadow puppet has to stay in a straight line from lens to screen in order for the change to be effective.

4. *Stage-to-stage transformation:* Raise the first character from the projection stage to underneath the reflecting lens. Place the second figure just below the first character. Move out the first character and lower the second figure to the stage.

Walking Screen Shadow Puppets

When students want the fully jointed legs of their screen shadow puppets to walk, it seems like a good idea to attach control rods to them. However, they're impossible to use without a second puppeteer.

The best alternative is to hold the figure's main support and arm rod in one hand and move one of its legs with the other. (See fig. 8.12.) To do this, place the shadow puppet on the shadow screen frame so that its legs have resistance for knee and hip movement. Then, clipping the front foot between the index and middle fingers, slide the foot forward along the frame. When the foot is extended, bring the rest of the puppet's body forward and repeat (or reverse) if necessary. (Make sure to attach a short length of string or yarn behind the figure's knees to prevent the legs from bending the wrong way.)

Fig. 8.12.

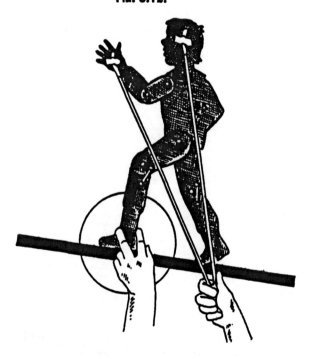

If this process is used for more than a few steps, the puppet looks as if it is limping or skipping. To avoid this, keep the puppet's feet slightly below the screen frame for a long walk or run. This technique is possible with overhead projector puppets, although their smaller joints require accurate cutting and more practice.

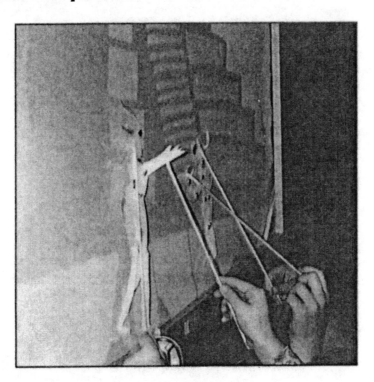

Partial Projector Puppets

Unlike hand puppets, which instantly change action and mood with the movement of unseen fingers, shadow puppets can't go beyond a set range of motion and emotion. A good example is Chapter 6's "Humpty-Dumpty" (fig. 6.7). Because the same puppet is unable to change expressions from ignorant bliss to pained surprise, two versions of the character become necessary.

When different versions of the same character have to be made, take a moment to determine if the entire figure is necessary. If it's going to be used against the shadow screen, the answer is usually yes. But if it's destined for the overhead projector, the answer is often no.

We frequently use partial projector puppets comprising only the section (i.e., an upper body, a head with moving mouth) necessary to complete a certain action. (See fig. 8.13, page 170.) This saves construction time and prompts more efficient rehearsal and performance.

Fig. 8.13.

ALTERNATIVE SHADOW FIGURES

Acetate Silhouettes

One of the first shadow sequences for "The Golden Candelabra" demanded that a princess fall from a tower window. (See fig. Pref. 3.) The scene was brief but vital. It had to be totally believable.

A screen shadow puppet didn't work; its shadow was far too big and showed through that of the projected tower. An overhead projector puppet stayed hidden behind the tower, but its size and control rod still drew too much attention.

The solution was to cut a small silhouette from contact paper and place it on a .005 millimeter acetate strip. (See fig. 8.14.) Only an inch long, the easily concealed silhouette sailed smoothly through the tower window, its small size allowing an impressive fall.

Acetate silhouettes are very useful as bridges between screen and projector shadow puppets, appearing momentarily in awkward scenes where the others can't be used effectively. They're also handy when a number of characters gather as a crowd or share a common action. For instance, "The Brementown Musicians" has a scene wherein the animal heroes climb on each other's backs to crash into a house of thieves. It's much easier to create an acetate strip of these animals than to orchestrate a pile of puppeteers and puppets. (They do have to be well drawn and cut, however. Any inaccuracies will be greatly magnified on the overhead projector.)

Although not as visually intrusive as control rods, acetate strips still show. To minimize this, trim the plastic from around the silhouettes as much as possible. Also, if an acetate figure travels in an arc (see fig. 8.15) (a flying bird or a shepherd walking over a mountain), it can be attached to the transparency scene with a brass paper fastener, much like Baby Bear's chair in the living room scene (fig. 7.9) of "Goldilocks and the Three Bears."

Fig. 8.14.

Fig. 8.15.

Profile Masks

Sometimes, only an actual person can accomplish the actions necessary in a story. While rehearsing a Grimm Brothers battle between a heroic prince and a fierce dragon, we initially used a screen shadow puppet prince against a partial projector puppet dragon. The dragon moved beautifully, but the prince looked like he was swatting flies.

Recognizing that more realistic movement was necessary, I stepped in as the prince. The battle looked much better, but now the prince had glasses and male pattern baldness.

The answer to this dilemma was a profile mask. I drew a much larger version of the prince's head on foam board (easily worked Styrofoam sheets sandwiched between layers of sturdy white paper), cut it out, and hot-glued a 2"-x-4" Velcro patch to it. Then I made a headband of webbing with a Velcro closure and another Velcro patch where the side of my head would be. (See fig. 8.16.)

Fig. 8.16.

After strapping on the headband behind the shadow screen, I put the foam board head into place and . . . voila! I was instantly transformed into the handsome prince! (See fig. 8.17.)

Fig. 8.17.

When rehearsing and performing with these flat masks, your head must stay absolutely parallel to the shadow screen. In so doing, only the mask's profile will be seen. Any turn will instantly reveal an actor with a piece of cardboard stuck to his head. If the blocking dictates a turn, exit toward the side you're facing and then turn around offstage and reenter. (The mask will be just as effective away from the screen.) During rehearsals and performances, regularly glance to the side to see if your profile is extending beyond the mask.

To make sure that the profile mask is the proper size, trace the character's head on a transparency first. Then tape foam board to the wall and project the outline on it. (See fig. 8.18.) Step into the projection and have an assistant adjust the projector until the tracing is slightly larger than your head. Then mark the outline on the foam board.

Fig. 8.18.

If in doubt as to size, make the mask bigger than necessary and trim it later. Also, be careful not to unbalance the mask with a huge nose or overwhelming hat. Because the profile is fastened at a single point, weighty items like these can cause the entire mask to twist off the Velcro patch.

9

Intermediate Projected Scenery Techniques for Ages Eight to Twelve

As noted in the introduction, most children come to school with a trained eye for the visual language of film and television. Students will immediately recognize the similarities between these two-dimensional electronic media and shadow puppetry. Some of the projected scenery effects introduced earlier approach cinematic conventions (the smooth fading of scene changes and the shifts of perspective when characters move from shadow screen to overhead projector, for instance). This chapter introduces some new techniques that further this visual kinship.

ROLLING PROJECTED SCENERY

Previously, we've used projections of single objects to create the illusion of movement on the shadow screen: a strip of lace for the horizontal run of joggers (fig. 5.19) and the vertical drop of someone falling from a building (fig. 5.20), as well as a twig for ascent and descent in "Jack and the Beanstalk" (fig. 5.23). Much more varied and detailed moving scenery is possible by using the acetate roll attachments available on many overhead projectors.

These optional rollers usually carry a 10"-wide strip of .003 clear acetate across the projection stage. (See fig. 9.1, page 176.) Instead of homework assignments, these rolls can be filled with extended lengths of scenery to provide panoramic views, movement areas between transparency scenes, and enough room for chases.

The only drawback to these rollers is their narrow diameter: The acetate winds into a tight cylinder, and the rather fragile .003 film must be used because thicker gauges unwind like clocksprings. Also, all scenery must be drawn because any applied material (such as transparent Form-X film) gets so tightly wound that it wrinkles. The only solution is to create a wider-diameter roller system so that sturdier acetate and additional scenery materials can be used. Directions for two roller systems are in Chapter 11. For now, though, let's take a look at getting started with the basics.

Storyboarding

It's always best to plan rolling scenery in advance, even when the story is a simple one. (Transparency scenes can be quickly reshuffled if out of order, but a wrongly placed scene within an acetate roll requires surgery to remove and place elsewhere.) Called storyboarding, this process involves breaking the story down into scenes, then deciding which scenes roll and which stay static as transparencies.

Fig. 9.1.

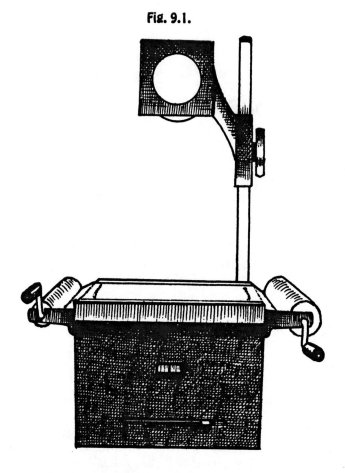

Because "The Three Little Pigs" in Chapter 6 has very few visuals (to prevent young scene changers from getting the pigs' projected houses caught in transparencies) and a lot of action, it's an excellent candidate for rolling projected scenery. The following scene breakdown also includes brief notations of action that prevent confusion when a scene gets used more than once.

1. Title ("The Three Little Pigs")

2. Hills (story intro and pigs' entrance)

3. Meadow (straw house by 1st pig)

4. Meadow (stick house by 2nd pig)

5. Meadow (brick house by 3rd pig)

6. Forest Scene (wolf intro)

7. Meadow (straw house blowdown and 1st pig exit)

8. Meadow (stick house blowdown and 2nd pig exit)

9. Meadow (attempted blowdown of brick house; wolf jumps to roof)

10. Brick House Interior (wolf falls into pot)

11. Hills (3rd pig triumphant or three pigs reunite; the end)

For the storyboard, follow a format similar to that charted in figure 9.2, which begins at the top and reads right to left. Draw a couple of parallel lines about two inches apart across a piece of notebook paper to represent the acetate roll. Then connect the lines on the right to indicate the beginning of the roll, which attaches to the corresponding stage-left roller of the projector.

Fig. 9.2.

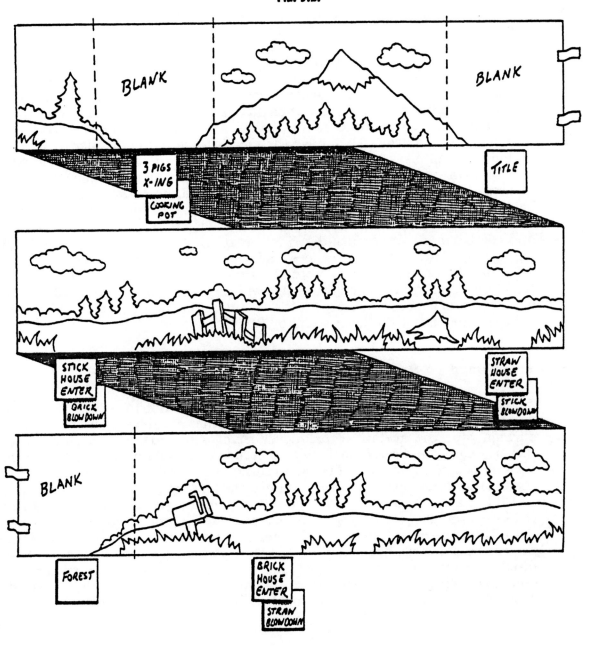

Mark "blank" to the left of this line. This is a reminder to leave at least a foot of empty acetate for connection to the roller and a clear space on the projection stage. This vacant area accommodates the title transparency (#1) boxed below the roll. Then draw a dotted line to the left of the blank and begin sketching the scenery of hills (#2).

Graduated views begin and end rolling scenes more naturally than straight-edged ones, so introduce hills of progressive height. Once on fully, the scene should run for at least a foot before the hills diminish in size. Although the projection stage measures only ten inches across, the shortest rolling scenes should be twelve inches long (plus graduated beginnings and endings) to supply margins for error.

Draw a dotted line to the left of the departing hills and mark a blank space for the close-up entrance of the three pigs. Indicate this below the roll as you did for the title transparency. To the left of the blank, introduce the meadow where they build their homes.

Once the meadow is on completely, sketch a stump or fencepost to note where the scenery should stop rolling for the entrance of the straw house (#3). Indicate this occurrence beneath the roll also. Then move a foot to the left and draw a similar landmark to denote where the stick house comes in (#4). Mark it underneath the roll; then go twelve inches to the left once more. Sketch another landmark to indicate where the brick house enters (#5), and note that below as well. Then have the meadow gradually disappear. Draw a dotted line and mark a blank for the arrival of the forest transparency (#6).

This transparency marks the point where the rolling scenery goes into reverse. After the wolf is introduced, the last landmark (not the one at the beginning of the roll) can be used for the blowdown of the straw house (#7). Then the middle landmark indicates the blowdown of the stick house (#8), and the beginning landmark denotes the attempted blowdown of the brick house (#9). Note these occurrences underneath the acetate as well.

After the wolf jumps to the roof, the blank space that originally contained the close-up entrance of the three pigs will host the cooking pot (#10), which can be part of a more elaborate interior scene. After the wolf's defeat, the hills will get rolled in for the joyous ending (#11).

From Storyboard to Scenery Roll

The .003 acetate is rather flimsy, so take care not to tear or wrinkle it during the marking and inking process. Rather than work with constant curling, tape the acetate to a long sheet of white art paper. This makes measurements and colors more visible. It also makes it possible to sketch the scenery on the white paper first so that it can be double-checked for correct scene order and lengths before tracing it on the acetate.

If the acetate roll runs out before the planned scenery, join it to a new roll by overlapping the edges by an inch and covering both with tape. (See fig. 9.3.) This prevents the new roll from getting caught on the side of the projection stage. To cover the join, ink in a tall opaque item (like a tree or building) from top to bottom. (If black transparency markers don't provide enough coverage, use contact paper or white Form-X film. The tightly wound roll will forgive this one addition for the sake of guaranteed opacity.)

Fig. 9.3.

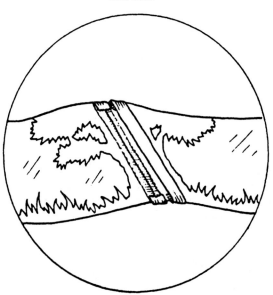

Remember that a rectangular shadow screen will not accommodate the entire scene cast by a square projection stage. (See fig. 2.13.) It's worthwhile to set up the overhead projector and screen to see how much top area of the scene roll will be lost as "spill." Then adjust the drawing accordingly.

Rehearsal and Performance with Rolling Scenery

Because of image reversal, rolling scenery traverses the shadow screen in the opposite direction from its motion on the overhead projector. For instance, the "Three Little Pigs" scenery initially rolls stage left on the projector but moves stage right on the screen. (This has been taken into account so that the story can be blocked and narrated almost the same way as in Chapter 6. However, rather than lifting the pigs' houses up out of focus after they're built, move them along with the rolling scenery until they've exited the projection stage. Reenter them the same way for the blowdowns, too. The effect is much more believable.)

Like a camera pan, rolling scenery should move at a slow or moderate pace so that the viewing audience can keep up with it. Even chase scenes should not advance at breakneck speed. Generally, "distant" characters (like acetate silhouettes) require less scenery operated at a slower speed for pursuits than do their "closer" counterparts (whole or partial projector puppets), which demand more scenery rolled at a faster clip.

Rolling scenery should also advance smoothly, especially when beginning or ending movement. This not only gives puppeteers a moment to prepare their figures but supports the audience's "willing suspension of disbelief" in the show. Viewers used to the seamless transitions of film and television notice jerky scene movement immediately.

Screen puppeteers must pay close attention to the scenery and activate their characters when it begins to roll. A gentle bobbing in place is necessary to give the impression of covering ground. (Remaining still gives a floating or gliding effect, which is effective only for ghosts, balloons, and heavily sedated flying creatures.) It also helps to face in the right direction.

Overhead projector puppeteers should bob their figures when scenery moves, too. They should also be careful when entering or exiting the projection stage so that their puppets don't get caught in the rollers. That can be a real showstopper!

USING TWO OVERHEAD PROJECTORS

For the variety of visuals and scene transitions already presented, most productions need only one overhead projector. But using two isn't difficult, and their dual action can provide instant scene changes for enhanced continuity as well as some impressive special effects.

Instant Scene Changes

The projectors should be placed next to each other with enough room between them to accommodate the comfortable operation of puppets and scenery. This will require angling the projectors slightly inward to ensure that the light from each covers the screen completely. (See fig. 9.4.)

Fig. 9.4.

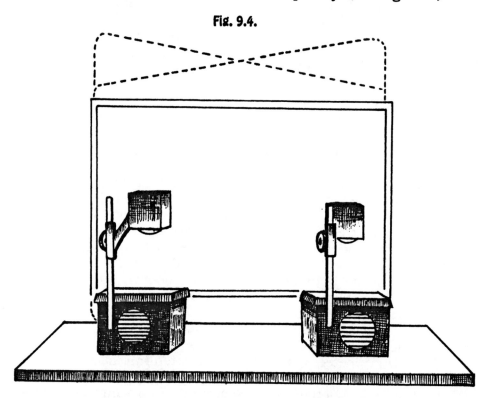

This angling will cause some "keystoning," a distortion wherein the projection cast furthest from the machine widens and lengthens. Circles tend to flatten into ellipses, and the use of student shadows and profile masks might need adjustment to the different light angle. Other than that, the irregularities are minimal.

As usual, it's better to practice a new technique before rehearsal. First, alternate transparency scenes between projectors. Place the first scene on the stage-right projector and the second scene on the stage-left projector. Then turn on the first scene. To change, flip the power switches of both machines simultaneously, turning the first scene off and the second scene on. (If the change isn't precise, that's all right. However, it's less jarring to have two scenes momentarily on at once rather than have the screen go dark.)

If the power switches are difficult to get to, poster paper "curtains" can be used in front of the reflecting lenses, descending to black out the first scene and ascending to reveal the second scene. With a bit more practice, they can also be used horizontally for side-to-side "wipes" between scenes. (See fig. 9.5.) These more gradual transitions take the pressure off student projector operators having a hard time being "simultaneous."

Fig. 9.5.

After a projector goes dark, remember to place the next transparency on it. With scene changes split between two machines, this step sometimes gets forgotten.

Light Overlays

In this technique, one overhead projector casts a scene while the other adds a brighter visual effect to it. (Unlike instant scene changes, wherein both projectors are angled, the projector with the main scene shoots straight ahead. Only the effects projector is angled.)

For example, lightning (fig. 5.38) can flash within a stormy night projection, and ghostly eyes (fig. 5.39) or mouths (fig. 5.40) can lurk within a gloomy haunted house. (See fig. 9.6.)

For a soft-edged fog or mist, slightly raise the fog pattern above the projection stage so that it's projected out of focus. The previous ghostly effects can also be introduced this way. (See fig. 9.7.) Convincing fire can be achieved by placing a flame pattern on the projection stage, adding orange Roscolux to the reflecting lens, and holding a water pan (fig. 5.24) between them. The water movement distorts the projection into flamelike flickers.

Fig. 9.6.

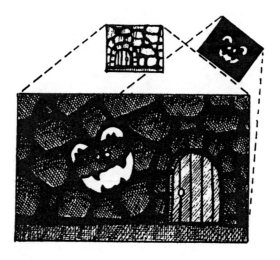

Fig. 9.7.

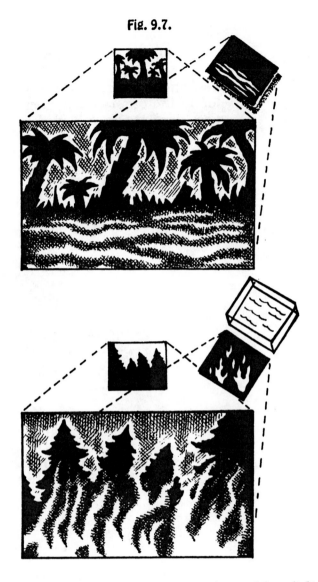

Some movement of light overlays is achieved by sliding the effect around on the projection stage. Much more is possible with the overhead projector attached to a swivel base or lazy Susan. (Use wide masking tape or duct tape to anchor the projector to the swivel, as in figure 9.8, page 184. For extra security, also tape the base of the swivel to the tabletop.)

Fig. 9.8.

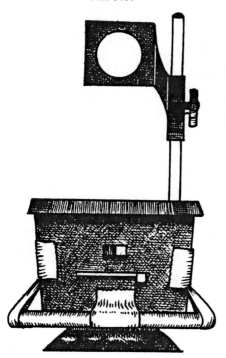

Now fast-moving illuminated objects like meteors and comets are feasible. (See fig. 9.9.) Simply place the effect on the projector and rotate the machine from one side to the other. Remember to moderate the effect's speed so that the audience can follow it.

One of our favorite production effects using a swiveled light overlay is a ghostly white Viking ship that slowly sails along an icy river until it reaches a waterfall, whereupon it continues gliding into the night sky.

Fig. 9.9.

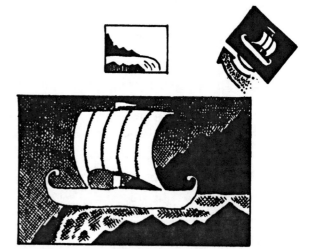

10

Production, Rehearsal, and Performance with Ages Eight to Twelve

Now that the students are older, they are more capable of handling their own puppets and scenery, as well as scene changes, narration, music, and sound effects. This is a wide age range, though, so the transition from a teacher-centered production to a totally student-operated one will be gradual. The teacher is the best judge as to what a class can handle in scope and independent work; please feel free to modify the following procedure for production, rehearsal, and performance with older children.

PRODUCTION BREAKDOWN

Although a story's individual scenes were noted for storyboarding in Chapter 9, a more complete production breakdown is necessary to identify all the tasks that translate the tale into a full-fledged show. The categories of a production breakdown follow.

1. *Puppets:* Whether major or minor, all characters should be listed. A large or repetitive cast can be reduced to simplify things, however. For instance, the abusive animal owners in "The Brementown Musicians" are often referred to rather than shown in student productions.

   Make sure to record the number of characters in variable or expandable roles. An example is the thieves in "The Brementown Musicians." The story doesn't specify how many, so note the number your class can comfortably play (Thief 1, Thief 2, etc.). If a cast needs to be padded with incidental characters, make sure they're listed too. (Bird 1, Bird 2, etc.)

2. *Props:* These comprise anything a character uses.

3. *Scenery:* Catalog all necessary scenes with an eye toward simplification. Consider dropping unimportant locations and playing brief scenes against a screen filled only with colored light.

4. *Overhead projector operators:* No more than two students per projector are necessary to change scenes.

5. *Narrators:* Although some lines might be spoken by puppeteers, one or two narrators are needed for exposition.

6. *Music and sound effects creators:* A number of students can be used to supply music and sound effects with simple percussion instruments such as tambourines, wood blocks, ratchets, and xylophones.

The first three categories are dictated by the story; the latter three are determined by student ability and the level of complexity you'd like to pursue.

ASSIGNING PRODUCTION TASKS

Make sure the students are familiar with the story; then write the entire production breakdown on the blackboard and assign jobs to students in the same order.

1. *Puppets:* Go through the list of characters and ask for volunteers. Should a role remain unfilled, go on and return to vacancies after all categories have been offered.

   Because some classes engage in a staggering amount of deal making and character swapping, inform students that they must notify you if they want to change roles after assignment. This prevents enormous confusion when directing, especially when students are absent. In addition, let them know that puppeteers can hold no other positions during production, rehearsal, and performance.

2. *Props:* Those making a prop must work with the person whose puppet is using it. This ensures a workable relative size and method of operation. Because props are usually operated by puppeteers, propmakers can be reassigned to minor or incidental puppet characters. Jobs as overhead projector operators, narrators, and music and sound effects creators are also open to them.

3. *Scenery:* Because scenery makers must give up their transparencies to the overhead projector operators, they can also receive new tasks as minor or incidental character puppeteers, narrators, overhead projector operators, and music and sound effects creators. It's perfectly fine for several students to work together on a scene

4. *Narrators:* Skilled readers with strong, easily understood voices need to be chosen for this assignment. Because they are not used during production, narrators can assist with props or scenery.

5. *Overhead projector operators:* Two attentive and well-organized students are needed for changing scenes. Again, they can be assigned to props or scenery during production.

6. *Music and sound effects creators:* Whether these students engage in additional work during production depends solely on the complexity of musical accompaniment. Simple percussive music and sound effects usually allow time for additional work in props or scenery.

After going through all the categories, return to unfilled positions and assign unemployed students.

REHEARSAL AND PERFORMANCE SETUP

Assuming the use of narrators, overhead projector operators, and music and sound effects creators, rehearsals and performances can be organized as in figure 10.1.

Fig. 10.1.

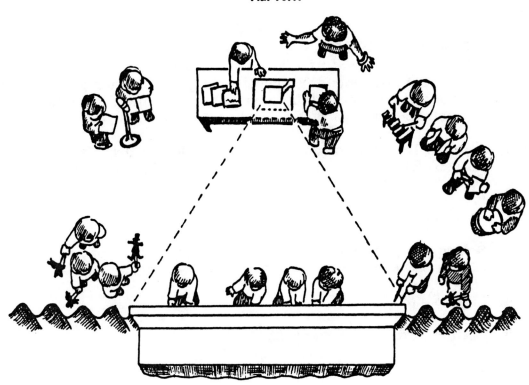

As the initial blocking of a show can take some time, students whose participation is momentarily unneeded can go back to their seats. But as rehearsals take more finished form, puppeteers and overhead projector operators should get used to staying backstage for the duration of a show.

Young narrators get worn out with the repetition of stop-and-start blocking; it's best for them to stay seated until the show has assumed its basic form. Narrators can remain backstage if they are to perform in the classroom or use a microphone in an auditorium. It's easier to keep an eye on the shadow screen for cues, and light spill from the overhead projector is usually enough to read by (although an additional source can certainly be added). In a larger room without a sound system, narrators have no choice but to work in front of the audience. (Stage curtains block sound almost as much as sight.) If such is the case, they should get used to the position from the beginning.

The musicians and sound effects creators should also stay in their seats until the first blocking is complete. Distribute instruments only after a show is roughed in, as it's impossible to stop unsupervised fingers from tapping (and dropping) cymbals, drums, and other migraine-producing percussion gadgets. (Ideally, the music teacher would work separately with this group.) When the production is ready for music and sound effects, these performers should assemble and stay in their assigned area.

Now, we'll put this process to the test with the presentation of a couple of stories.

STORIES

"The Brementown Musicians"

■*Production:* As students finish constructing the following puppets, props, and scenery, check them off the production breakdown. Invite the children to demonstrate their finished products on the shadow screen.

1. *Puppets:* Donkey, Donkey Owner, Dog, Dog Owner, Cat, Cat Owner, Rooster, Rooster Owner, Thief 1, Thief 2, Thief 3, Thief 4, acetate silhouette of stacked animals

2. *Props:* none

3. *Scenery:* title, farm scene 1, farm scene 2, road scene 1, road scene 2, house exterior scene, house interior scene, sunrise-sunset strip

4. *Narrators (2)*

5. *Overhead projector operators (2)*

6. *Musicians and sound effects creators (4)*

As with all previous productions, transparency scenes are indicated. However, this story could also be produced with rolling scenery. A storyboard like the one introduced earlier (fig. 9.2) is charted in figure 10.2. It can be used with the following stage directions with only minimal adjustments.

After you have given students their assignments, it's time to begin.

Fig. 10.2.

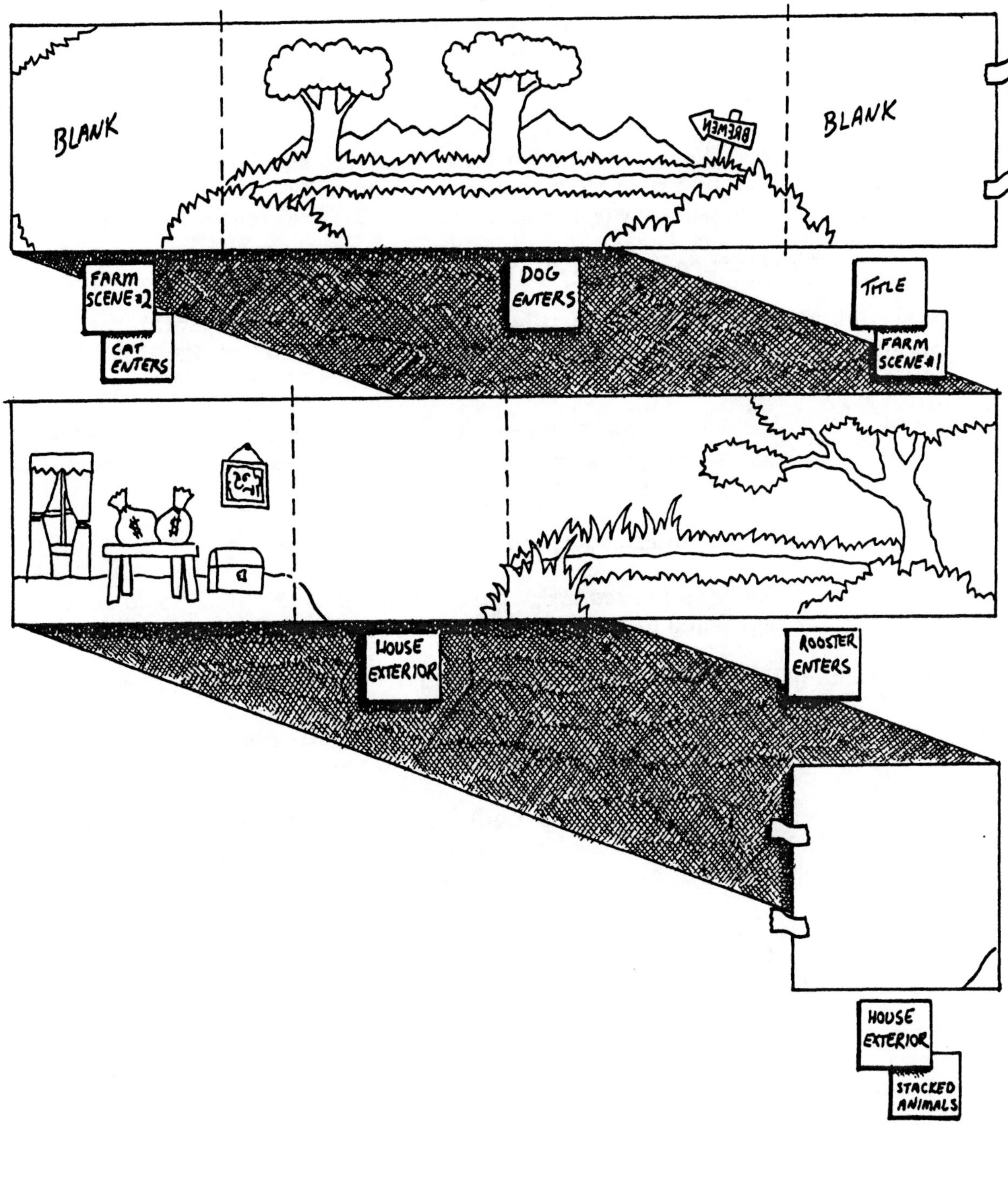

BLANK

BREMEN

BLANK

FARM
SCENE #2

CAT
ENTERS

DOG
ENTERS

TITLE

FARM
SCENE #1

HOUSE
EXTERIOR

ROOSTER
ENTERS

HOUSE
EXTERIOR

STACKED
ANIMALS

■*Rehearsal:* Ask narrators, musicians, and sound effects creators to take their seats while puppeteers and overhead projector operators begin initial blocking. Have the overhead projector operators gather the transparency scenes and stack them in order of appearance. Place the reversed title card on the projector.

The Donkey, Dog, Cat, and Rooster puppeteers should kneel stage right. Operators of the animal owners should kneel stage left in the same order.

Check the preset. Lower the curtain; then lift it to reveal the title.

The Brementown Musicians

Change scenes from the title to farm scene 1. (Incidental barnyard animals can enter and exit at this point.) Donkey enters stage right and crosses to center screen.

> *Once upon a time, there was an old donkey. He had worked very hard for many years. But now that he could no longer pull a cart, his owner wanted to be rid of him.*

Donkey Owner enters stage left and crosses to Donkey.

> *"Miserable creature," said his owner. "All you do is cost me money. Enjoy the day, for it will be your last."*

Donkey Owner turns and exits stage left.

> *"Well, there's no future for me here," thought the donkey. So he left the farm he had always known and started on the road to Bremen.*

Donkey turns and exits stage right. Change scenes from farm scene 1 to road scene 1. Donkey operator steps to overhead projector and enters Donkey on projection stage from stage left, stopping at center stage.

> *"Hee-haw! Hee-haw!" he cried. "What a fine voice I have! I know what I shall do. I shall go to Bremen and become a fine musician. There I shall make my fortune!"*

As Donkey exits the projector stage from stage right, Dog enters the shadow screen from stage right and crosses to center. The Donkey operator returns to kneeling stage right at the shadow screen.

> *Up ahead, an old dog stood shivering in the road. He had served his master well for many years. But now that he could no longer hunt or herd, the master had no use for him.*

Dog Owner enters stage left and crosses to Dog.

> *"Mangy cur!" snarled the owner. "Away with you!"*

As Dog Owner exits stage left, Donkey enters stage right. Dog turns to face him.

> *"Why are you so sad?" asked the donkey.*
> *"I am old and useless," said the dog. "My master no longer wants me!"*
> *"Let me hear your voice," said the donkey.*
> *"Woof! Woof! Woof!" barked the dog.*
> *"What a lovely voice!" cried the donkey. "You are far from useless. Come with me to Bremen where we will become great musicians!"*
> *The dog agreed and off they went.*

Dog turns and both exit stage left. (Donkey could do a crossover to take the lead here. If he continues in front, though, the crossovers will become increasingly difficult as more animals join the procession.) Change scenes from road scene 1 to farm scene 2. Cat enters stage right and crosses to center while Cat Owner enters stage left.

> *Not far away, an old cat was having a difficult time.*
> *"Worthless animal!" said his owner. "You haven't caught a mouse in months. You had best be gone!"*

Cat Owner exits stage left. After a beat, Donkey and Dog enter stage left.

> *"I have never seen such an unhappy cat," said the donkey. "What is the matter?"*
> *"I am old and slow," said the cat. "My master has ordered me to leave."*
> *"Pray let me hear your voice," said the donkey.*
> *"Meow! Meow! Meow!" said the cat.*
> *"Absolutely beautiful!" cried the donkey. "Please come with us to Bremen where we will become fine musicians!"*
> *The cat agreed and off they went.*

Cat turns and all animals exit stage right. Change scenes from farm scene 2 to road scene 2. Rooster enters stage right and crosses to center screen. Rooster Owner enters stage left.

> *Meanwhile, an old rooster was losing his home.*
> *"You are nothing but dust and feathers!" said his owner. "Off with you!"*

Rooster Owner exits stage left. Donkey, Dog, and Cat enter stage right. Rooster turns to face them.

> *"Proud rooster!" called the donkey. "Why aren't you crowing to greet the day?"*
> *"Alas," sighed the rooster. "This day I have lost everything!"*
> *"Let me hear your voice," said the donkey.*
> *"Cock-a-doodle-doo!" crowed the rooster.*
> *"An astounding instrument!" declared the donkey. "You must join our band. We are going to Bremen to become great musicians."*
> *The rooster agreed and off they went.*

All animals exit stage right. Donkey, Dog, Cat, and Rooster puppeteers then come to the projector and enter the characters onto the projection stage from stage left to stage right.

> *The road was long and winding, so the animals sang to pass the time.*
> *"Hee-haw! Hee-haw!" brayed the donkey.*
> *"Woof! Woof! Woof!" barked the dog.*
> *"Meow! Meow! Meow!" meowed the cat.*
> *"Cock-a-doodle-doo!" crowed the rooster.*

As Cat and Rooster cross and exit, slowly lower the sunrise-sunset strip (figs. 5.11 and 5.13) in front of the reflecting lens for nighttime. Change scenes from road scene 2 to the house exterior scene as the animal puppeteers kneel stage left. (The house should be projected on the stage-right side of the shadow screen.) Donkey enters stage left and crosses to the house as the other animals hang back, also stage left.

> *As darkness fell, the animals saw a house before them.*
> *"I shall see if we can spend the night here," said the donkey. "The owners will be thrilled to have such fine musicians for company."*
> *He peeked in the window. "Goodness gracious!" he cried.*

Donkey turns and runs back to his friends.

> *"There's a cutthroat band of thieves inside!" he whispered to his friends.*

As the animals exit stage left, change from the exterior house scene to the interior house scene. Have puppeteers operating thieves 1 and 2 kneel stage left while those moving thieves 3 and 4 kneel stage right. All thieves enter when the scene change is complete. All animal operators step up to stage left of the projector.

> *Indeed, there was. The table was heaped with the money and jewels they had stolen. The thieves laughed wickedly as they bragged about their terrible crimes.*
> *"Haw! Haw!" roared one. "We shall live like kings!"*
> *"Dirty, rotten crooked kings!" laughed another.*
> *The Brementown Musicians heard everything.*
> *"This is not right," said the donkey. "I have an idea!"*

Thieves exit the way they entered as the scene changes from the interior house scene to a blank blue screen. Donkey enters stage left on the projector, then slides down to make room for Dog on his back.

> *"Dog, my good friend," said the donkey. "Climb upon my back!"*

Donkey exits off the bottom of the projection stage as Dog slides down to make room for Cat.

> *"Now, Cat!" said the donkey. "Leap up on Dog!"*

Dog exits the bottom of the projection stage as Cat slides down to make room for Rooster.

"And finally, Rooster," said the donkey. "Fly up and perch on Cat! Then sing for all you're worth!"

As Rooster and the still visible Cat exit stage right, lower the exterior house scene into focus. Enter the acetate silhouette of stacked animals from stage right on the projection stage. The animals should first make noises individually, then as a group.

The donkey brayed. The dog barked. The cat meowed. And the rooster crowed.

Then a wobbly tower of braying, barking, meowing, crowing animals moved toward the house.

"What is that horrible noise?" cried the thieves.

Move the stacked-animals acetate through the window and exit it stage left. Change scenes from the exterior house scene to the interior house scene. The thieves reenter from previous positions, running and turning about as the stacked-animals acetate reenters stage left and bounds around the projection stage. After some bedlam . . .

The thieves screamed in fright when the Brementown Musicians crashed into the house. The donkey kicked. The dog bit. The cat scratched. And the rooster clawed. It was all too much for the robbers. They fled in terror.

All thieves exit as before. Change scenes from the house interior scene (including the stacked-animals acetate) to road scene 2. All thieves reenter and face each other.

"What happened back there?" asked one thief.

"I don't know," moaned another. "It must have been a man-eating monster!"

"Whatever it was," cried a third, "I'm never going back there!"

"But what about our money?" said the fourth.

"It can have the money!" screamed the others. "Let's get out of here!"

All thieves exit as before while the scene changes from road scene 2 to the house interior scene. Raise the sunrise-sunset strip to make it daytime again. All animal operators kneel stage right and enter characters when the scene change is complete. Bring down the curtain as the narration ends.

"What a wonderful reward for our singing!" said the donkey.
"Truly!" said the dog. "A new home, lots of food, and bags of money!"
"And we didn't even get to Bremen," said the cat.
"We must be very fine musicians indeed!" crowed the rooster.
And the Brementown Musicians lived there happily ever after from that day to this. The end.

This simplified version of the story lacks the usual return of individual thieves to the house, where they're defeated one by one. This section can be added for the oldest performers; there's already a substantial amount for younger students of this age level to learn. As suggested previously, divide rehearsals into sections for easier memorization of blocking and lines. Make sure to review prior staging before tackling a new portion.

If puppeteers are going to deliver some of their character's lines, make sure they say them loudly enough for the audience to hear them. This goes for music and sound effects, too. After all, this is one of the very few times it's all right to be loud in school. So whoop it up!

Finally, rehearse a curtain call. The audience loves to applaud a job well done, and performers will be able to accept this approval more graciously with an organized bow.

■*Performance:* Assure students that all the work they have done in rehearsal will take care of them in performance. Note that attention will still be needed throughout the show by all concerned, on screen and off. Caution them not to get distracted by the projections, thereby missing cues or failing to get out of someone else's way.

Ask them to cover mistakes rather than draw attention to them. The audience (for whom all this work has been done) is ready and eager to be entertained. They are not interested in who fumbled a transparency or broke a puppet. They want to see the show.

Keep that roll of masking tape and some tabbed control rods nearby for emergency shadow puppet repair. As generals once surveyed their troops from hilltops, stay near the overhead projector to quietly correct or prompt your troupe.

■*Post-Performance Evaluation:* It's appropriate and worthwhile for older students to find out if their performances can be improved. But criticism has to be constructive and balanced with genuine praise for the individual efforts that constitute group success.

Viewing a videotaped performance can be helpful, as it makes shortcomings obvious without being personal. However, if someone has made a drastic error that he or she is all too aware of, spare the agony of a rerun.

If additional performances are slated, remind students that opportunities remain to correct mistakes and improve performances. Conversely, caution a wildly successful group not to get cocky.

"The Goblin Spiders"

■*Production:* This spooky traditional story from Japan is a great favorite among older students who'd like a break from the familiar folktales. Given that the numbers in expandable roles might need adjustment, the production breakdown is as follows:

1. *Puppets:* Tired Traveler 1, Tired Traveler 2, Friendly Priest 1, Friendly Priest 2, goblin spiders (expandable to eight), Headstrong Warrior 1, Headstrong Warrior 2, Mayor, villagers (expandable to four), Great Samurai, High Priest

2. *Props:* tray of food and drink, samisen (stringed instrument)

3. *Scenery:* title, temple exterior scene, web transparency, village scene, mountain scene, temple interior scene

4. *Narrators (2)*

5. *Overhead projector operators (expandable to 4 if two projectors used)*

6. *Musicians and sound effects creators (4)*

Older students can initiate cultural research on Japan (or other folktales' countries of origin) to gather authentic details for puppets and scenery, much of which can be tied in to other curricula.

A storyboard for rolling scenery (fig. 10.3, page 196) is offered as an alternative to the transparency scenes referred to in the following stage directions.

■*Rehearsal:* Overhead projector operators should stack transparency scenes (alternating them between projectors if two machines are used) and reverse the title for projection. Have both tired traveler puppeteers kneel stage right and both friendly priest puppeteers kneel stage left. Four goblin spider operators can stay low at the shadow screen; two more goblin spider operators flank the overhead projector, ready for a screen-to-screen transformation (fig. 8.11).

Fig. 10.3.

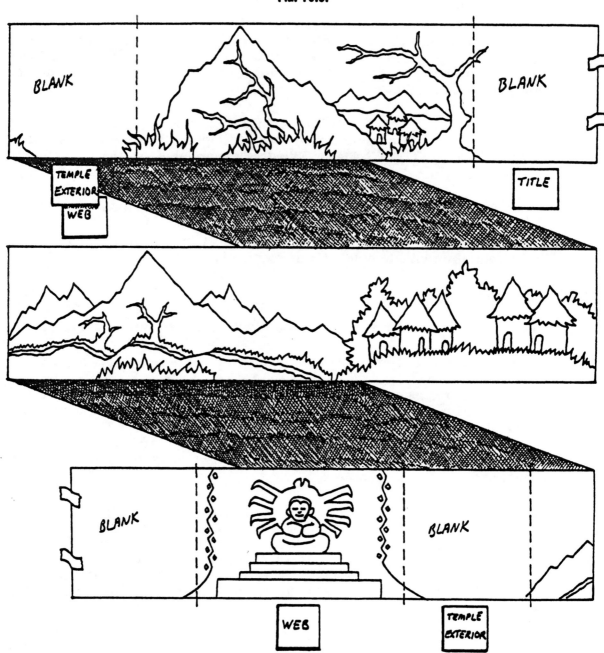

Lower the curtain; then raise it to reveal the title.

The Goblin Spiders

After the narrator has announced the title, the four goblin spiders enter from the bottom of the shadow screen and crawl over the letters. As the title goes out of focus prior to a scene change to the temple exterior scene, have the goblin spiders also go out of focus by drawing back from the screen to the projector. Upon their exit, complete the scene change.

Long ago in Japan, there was a haunted temple in the mountains above a village. During the day, it was safe enough, and tired travelers often rested there from their long journeys.

Both tired travelers enter stage right and cross to center.

Friendly priests brought the weary pilgrims food and water.

As the friendly priests enter stage left to meet them, slowly lower the sunrise-sunset strip to nighttime. Ready the web transparency for placement on the temple exterior scene.

But when night fell, the temple became the dreadful nesting place of many goblin spiders. Giant webs suddenly crisscrossed the temple gardens.

Quickly lower the web transparency onto the temple exterior scene.

The friendly priests transformed into their true shapes as monstrous goblin spiders!

Both friendly priests zip back to the reflecting lens and are replaced by the two goblin spiders in a screen-to-screen transformation. Once on the shadow screen, the goblin spiders noisily dispatch the tired travelers, and all parties exit the bottom of the screen. Tired traveler puppeteers should clear out from behind the screen while the goblin spider operators stay for the next victims.

Have both headstrong warriors ready to enter stage right one at a time.

At times, headstrong warriors would enter the temple, hoping to gain great glory from vanquishing the goblin spiders.

Headstrong Warrior 1 enters carefully stage right and crosses slowly to center, where he is done in by the lurking goblin spiders. Headstrong Warrior 2 enters in the same fashion and meets a similar doom. All exit bottom of screen and clear the area for other puppeteers.

But all met the same fate.

Raise the sunrise-sunset strip to daytime as scenes change from the temple exterior scene to the village scene. The mayor enters stage right as the villagers enter stage left to meet him center screen.

The villagers became tired of being terrorized by these terrible creatures. They called upon their mayor to do something. The mayor gazed at the citizens' fearful faces and had an idea. He would summon the Great Samurai to cleanse the temple of its horrible inhabitants.

The mayor and villagers exit the way they entered. The mayor puppeteer steps to the overhead projector and enters his character stage right on the projection stage. The Great Samurai enters stage left on the projection stage.

When the fearless Great Samurai arrived, the mayor told him what he must do. "Be careful of the priests of the temple," he counseled. "They look harmless enough, but the darkness of night will reveal them as goblin spiders!"
"Indeed!" The Great Samurai scoffed. "I am sure I can step on a few crawling spiders."
"Do not be so boastful," warned the mayor. "Many have been caught in their terrible webs and have never returned."
The Great Samurai considered the fear in the mayor's face and voice. "I will be alert," he said.

As the mayor and Great Samurai turn and exit the way they entered, change scenes from the village scene to the mountain scene. The Great Samurai enters the shadow screen stage left and crosses the mountains, exiting stage right.

That afternoon, the Great Samurai journeyed to the haunted temple.

Change scenes from the mountain scene to the temple exterior scene. The Great Samurai enters stage right. Both friendly priests enter stage left to meet him.

Friendly priests met him outside the temple and graciously offered him food and drink. They escorted him inside to meet the high priest. The Great Samurai could scarcely believe such helpful servants could be of harm.

Both friendly priests turn and exit stage left, followed by the Great Samurai. Change scenes from the temple exterior scene to the temple interior scene. The characters reenter stage left with the Great Samurai in front. The high priest enters stage right with the samisen and dismisses both friendly priests, who exit stage left.

Once inside, the Great Samurai was mightily swayed by the grace and concern of the high priest. He accepted food and drink from the little man and talked with him at length. The high priest played a beautiful melody on the samisen as the sun set.

Begin lowering the sunrise-sunset strip slowly.

> *At twilight, the high priest offered the samisen to the Great Samurai.*

The Great Samurai crosses to the high priest. The samisen is transferred. Ready the web transparency as the sunrise-sunset strip makes the scene nighttime.

> *Then night fell. Instantly, the samisen changed into a giant sticky web!*

Quickly lower the web transparency to the temple interior scene.

> *And the high priest changed into a huge goblin spider!*

Quickly enact a screen-to-screen transformation from high priest into goblin spider.

> *The Great Samurai fought as hard as he could, but his arms were hampered by the web. Again and again, he struck at the horrible beast. More goblin spiders entered to help their chief.*

With the Great Samurai turning about at center screen, enter more goblin spiders from both sides. Lift the web transparency as the hero cuts himself free.

> *The Great Samurai managed to cut himself free from the web. Spider after spider fell to his flashing blade.*

As the goblin spiders exit off the bottom of the screen, raise the sunrise-sunset strip to daytime.

> *By morning, the temple was cleansed of the goblin spiders.*

The Great Samurai exits stage left as the scene changes from the temple interior scene to the temple exterior scene. He reenters stage left as the mayor and villagers enter stage right. Lower the curtain as the narration ends.

> *The mayor and villagers clambered up the mountain to see with their own eyes the glorious victory of the Great Samurai. Never again would their village and temple be troubled by the terrible plague of goblin spiders. The end.*

It's essential that fight scenes not degenerate into extended rounds of puppet bashing. The battles should be kept brief by quickly concluding them after they reach a high point. This stems overexcitement on the part of puppeteers and prevents long periods of repetitive movement, which audiences soon tire of.

A longer conflict has to be visually interesting and emotionally engaging. This can be achieved only by choreographing specific movements amid varied settings or perspectives. Because the shadow puppets have limited motion, consider using student shadows with profile masks (fig. 8.17) in some scenes, perhaps in conjunction with rolling projected scenery (fig. 9.1).

And please remind students how they can avoid wrecking their creations (see traffic control hint 3 in Chapter 4 and figure 4.10).

■*Performance:* At this point, you're a veteran. Don't forget the curtain call, though!

■*Post-Performance Evaluation:* Most definitely.

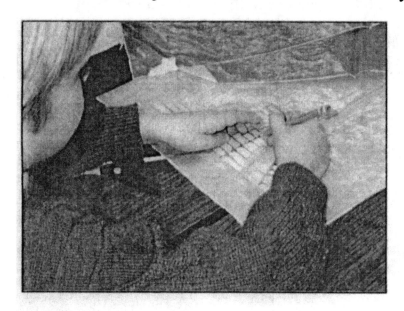

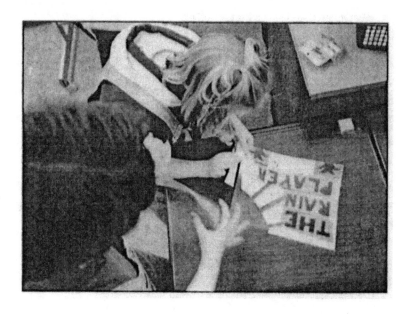

11

Advanced Projected Scenery Techniques

The following techniques are not beyond use in elementary productions but do require substantially more time to plan and construct, as well as careful supervision during rehearsal.

REFLECTED-LIGHT FIGURES

Some novel effects can be achieved by reflecting light off negative silhouettes on 12"-x-12" sheets of plexiglass mirror. (See fig. 11.1.) After completely covering the mirror with a low-tack contact paper or opaque Form-X film, draw a character on it. Cut the outline with an X-Acto knife and strip the character out, leaving a mirror silhouette.

Fig. 11.1.

The focused light of an overhead projector bounces off the mirror silhouette to the shadow screen, creating a ghostly white figure. (See fig. 11.2, page 202.) It will not have the brightness of a light overlay (figs. 9.6 and 9.7), but it can be wonderfully distorted by flexing the plexiglass. (Naturally, the effect looks best on a medium to dark scene.)

We've used this distortion for ghosts (flexing the mirrors so that flying apparitions turn in midair) and to introduce characters. (In "Peter and the Wolf," unrecognizable streams of light emerged from shadows of musical instruments, gradually expanding into the characters tunefully portrayed by them.)

This is not a difficult technique, but it does involve placing an overhead projector near the shadow screen to aim it backstage. The machine's blinding light, electrical cord, and boxy frame constitute tripping hazards that must be minimized. So a short list of precautions, also illustrated in figure 11.2, is presented on page 202.

Fig. 11.2.

1. Place cardboard shades around the projector to stop light spill as much as possible.

2. Turn the projector on only when necessary.

3. Have students shade their eyes with the plexiglass sheets while using them.

4. Use duct tape or wide masking tape to secure electrical cords to the floor.

5. Place the projector to the side of the screen as far as possible from traffic areas.

   Please don't use glass mirror under any circumstances. It doesn't bend and cracks into splinters very easily. Plexiglass mirror is a must.

USING THREE OVERHEAD PROJECTORS

Our larger productions frequently use three projectors either to create elaborate transitions and special effects on a single screen or to handle simultaneous projections on three screens. (See fig. 11.3.) The center projector has a wide-angle lens and handles the bulk of transparency scenes and rolling scenery. The others flank it and handle minor scenes, light overlays, and transitional effects. (If angling the side projectors toward a single screen, remember to adjust for the "keystoning" effect shown in fig. 9.4.)

Fig. 11.3.

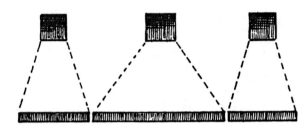

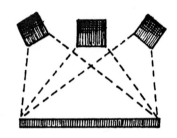

As productions become more complex and formal, consider using machines with bulb changers. It's incalculably easier to flip a switch or lever than to spend show-stopping minutes fixing a burnout.

An overhead projector is only a tool to transmit a visual. A production will not automatically improve by adding a machine. Before embarking on a triple-projector show, make sure that the full potential of one or two has been explored. Then decide on the complexity of the production, given the needs of the story and, more important, the abilities of your cast. Please don't allow Spielbergian visions to overwhelm the capacities of twelve-year-olds.

Other than these considerations, the option is open. It's now up to you to choose from the extensive range of scenic methods, materials, and transitions and combine them into a vital visual production.

POLARMOTION

Polarmotion is the trade name of a polarized self-adhesive plastic film that provides actual animated movement to overhead projections. When it is added to transparencies, rain falls, flames flicker, stars twinkle, and wheels revolve, all without manual control. Using Polarmotion isn't difficult, but explaining how it works is.

Imagine your class throwing Frisbees at a fence of vertical posts. The disks would approach the fence at many different angles. The only Frisbees to actually pass through the fence would be those that flew vertically, matching the openings between the posts. All the others would hit the fence and stop.

Similarly, the projector's beam of light travels in planes of various angles. A sheet of polarized plastic acts as the vertical fence, letting through the one plane of light that matches its own and stopping all others. (See fig. 11.4, page 204.)

Now, let's say that some disks get through and roll toward a gate that is constantly being opened and shut by an annoying four-year-old named Dexter. Should Dexter open the gate when the Frisbees arrive, they get through. If he shuts it, tough noogies.

A *rotating* sheet of polarized plastic acts as the gate, letting through the remaining plane of light only when their angles coincide. Because the sheet spins, the remaining light is alternately blocked and let through.

Fig. 11.4.

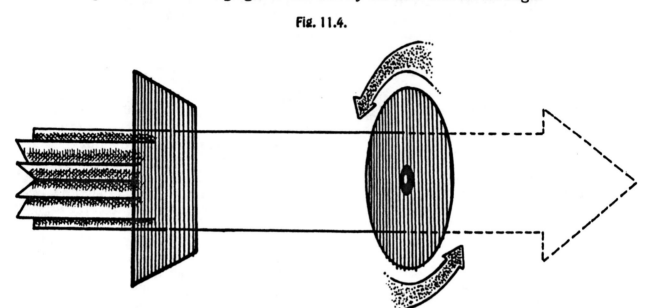

This basic process has been greatly elaborated by Polarmotion. The patterned polarized plastic applied to transparency scenes acts as the fence, and a spinning motorized wheel of polarized plastic clipped to the reflecting lens of the projector acts as the gate. With this twin polarization at work, the patterns in the transparency scenes alternately lighten and darken, creating an illusion of movement much like the "chaser lights" of movie theater marquees. (See fig. 11.5.)

Polarmotion is available from Frank Wooley & Company, Inc., 529 Franklin Street, Reading, PA 19602 (Tel: 610-374-8335, Fax: 610-374-3214). A free handbook-catalog and a price sheet are available upon request. Ordering a 3" hand-spinner of polarized plastic (#100-00 at $1.25) and demo plate of patterns (#399-00 at $1.25) is an inexpensive way to determine if the product is applicable to your production.

Price is a consideration with Polarmotion. Full sheets (16" x 24") of patterned motion material cost $49 each. Half-sheets (12" x 16") are available in some patterns for $26, as are quarter-sheets (8" x 11") for $14. The smallest sheets provide enough material for most scenes and almost completely cover the projection stage for full-screen effects.

Cutting the laminated layers of Polarmotion requires a strong hand. All cuts must be complete before stripping away the backing material. Otherwise, the motion material separates from the adhesive layer. Also, the adhesive grips immediately, so placement must be precise. (The handbook contains hints to surmount both these concerns.)

Fig. 11.5.

Fig. 11.6.

The motorized spinner (#109-10) is the costliest item, running $119.50 for a 115 VAC 60 Hz current unit with an 11" polarizing wheel. This assembly mounts to the side of the reflecting lens with a supplied self-stick Velcro patch. (See fig. 11.6.)

Besides being expensive, the polarizing wheel does reduce the light output of the overhead projector by about a third. This requires performance in as dark a room as possible for best viewing of the motion effects. (Rather than dim an entire show for the sake of a special effect, we either remove the polarizing wheel during scene changes or limit its use to one of the flanking projectors.)

Polarmotion also manufactures self-adhesive color tinting sheets in an array of thirty-nine colors. Full sheets (16" x 24" at $9.95 each) are almost twice as expensive as transparent Form-X film (although quarter-sheets measuring 8" x 11" are available for $2.75). Both varieties work well but must not be applied between the motion material and the polarizing spinner. Being optically active, they interfere with the smooth flow of the animation. To prevent this, fasten the motion material to the front of a transparency scene and any transparent color medium to the back.

ROLLING SCENERY RACKS

As mentioned earlier, the optional acetate rollers supplied with many overhead projectors require using .003 acetate wound to a narrow diameter. (See fig. 9.1.) This precludes the use of sturdier gauges of plastic and the application of additional scene materials such as wax paper, lace, Form-X film, and Polarmotion. Rolling scenery racks will allow these alternatives. They do take time and carpentry skill to make, however.

It will also be necessary to hand-cut the 10"-wide lengths of .005 or .0075 clear acetate used for the scenery rolls. Rolled acetate is usually available in 40"-wide rolls measuring 12, 50, or 100 feet. Cost ranges from approximately $20 (.005) and $30 (.0075) for 12' lengths to $75 (.005) and $105 (.0075) for 50' rolls.

To cut the rolls to size, mark a line 10 inches from the edge of an art table. With an assistant, unroll the acetate and align its edge with the table. Then use a metal straightedge and X-Acto blade to score the plastic along the line. It's not necessary to cut entirely through the film. A deep score followed by slight folding will provide a clean cut.

The following plans are for a single rack (one side-to-side scenery roll), a double rack (two side-to-side scenery rolls), and a triple rack (two side-to-side scenery rolls and a bottom-to-top roll for vertical effects).

All of the racks are constructed from 1"-x-2" finished lumber. Sections of closet pole are used for rollers, to which strips of 1"-thick foam rubber are added to increase their diameter. Because overhead projectors vary significantly in size and design, the directions will have to be adapted to the machines available to you.

Single Rolling Scenery Rack

This simple rack will handle most productions, including all the ones in this book.

■*Supplies:* approximately 12' of 1"-x-2" lumber, two 10½" lengths of closet pole, 1' of ½" dowel, ¾" wood screws, 1½" wood screws, 3' of 1½"-wide 1"-thick foam rubber, contact cement, electric drill, ½" drill bit, smaller bits for pilot holes, screwdriver, wood glue, 1' of 1"-x-2" board for handles, two screw-on or bolted knobs

■*Directions:* The basic construction of this rack is charted in figure 11.7, and a complete sketch is in figure 11.8, page 208.

Fig. 11.7.

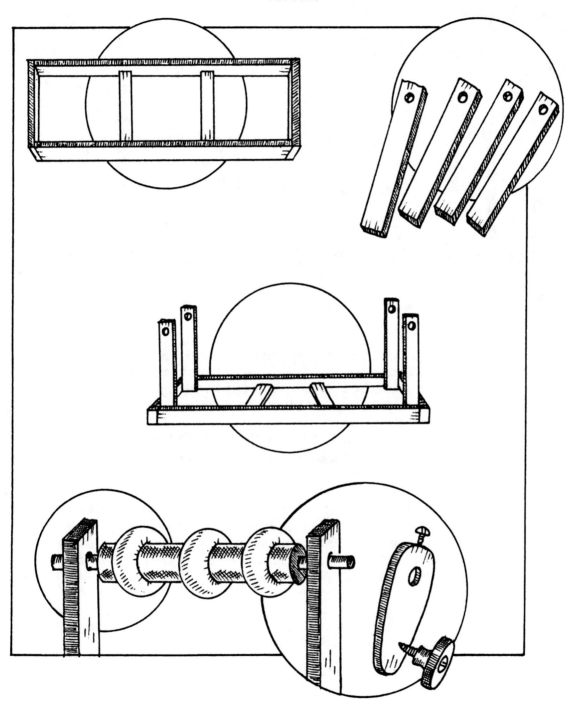

Fig. 11.8.

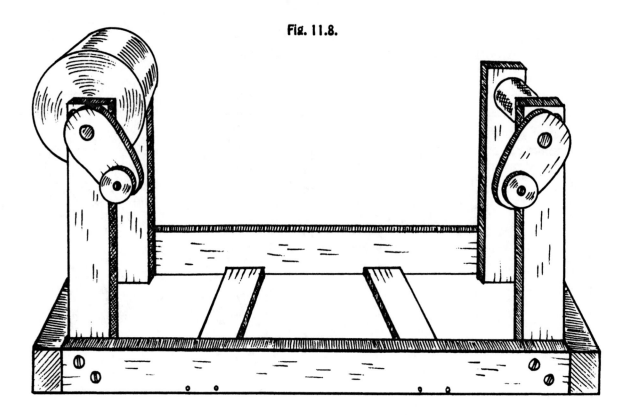

Measure the front base of the overhead projector, add approximately 18" to it, and cut two lengths of 1" x 2" lumber that size. Measure the side base of the projector, add 2" or 3" to it, and cut two lengths of 1" x 2" lumber to that size. Glue and screw these pieces on edge into a frame with the shorter pieces to the outside.

Cut four 1' lengths of 1" x 2". Center and drill a ½" hole 1½" from one end of each piece. Work the bit through these holes so that a ½" dowel will twist easily in them. Glue and screw the 1"-x-2" pieces upright in each corner with flat sides facing the length of the frame.

Center and drill ½"-wide holes about 1" deep in both ends of each 10½" length of closet pole. Cut four 3" lengths of ½" dowel. Glue one end of each dowel. Insert one in each piece of closet pole. After tapping it into place, slip it into the hole of the 1"-x-2" post. Align the other hole in the dowel with the hole in the opposite 1"-x-2" post. Insert the other glued dowel and tap it into place.

Cut two handles from the 1"-x-2" board. Drill a ½" hole near one end and attach knob at the other end. Glue end of protruding dowel and place handle over it. Add a setscrew to prevent twisting.

Cut three lengths of foam rubber for each closet pole, making sure they will encircle the pole completely. Apply contact cement to closet pole and attach foam rubber strips.

When attaching the 10"-wide acetate, roll it under the rollers rather than over. This pulls the plastic down toward the projection stage during operation, ensuring a sharp focus.

Double Rolling Scenery Rack

Two rolls afford an enormous amount of flexibility. Not only scenery can move from side-to-side; animals, vehicles, and characters applied to the second roll can traverse the screen in one direction while background scenery on the first roll slips by the other way. (See fig. 11.9.)

Fig. 11.9.

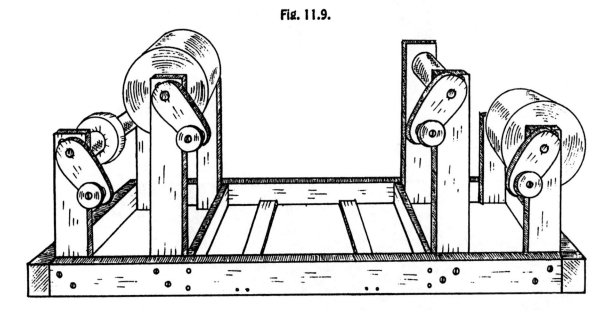

In most cases, we keep the bulk of our extended scenes on the roll moving stage left. All of the production storyboards in this book (figs. 9.2, 10.2, and 10.3) are oriented that way. The second roll contains shorter lengths of scenery and animal-vehicle-character crossings. This makes a longer show easier to memorize. Also, the screen or overhead projector puppets operating against this flow will move from audience left to audience right. Rather unconsciously, viewers expect this action because of the mechanics of reading.

To plan the second roll, set up a second storyboard that reads from the top left and down. (See fig. 11.10, page 210.) The most important aspect of planning is making sure that there are blank spaces between visuals in this second roll to allow projection of scenery from the first roll and transparency scenes. Without these 12"-to-15" gaps, there will be unwanted double projections.

Fig. 11.10.

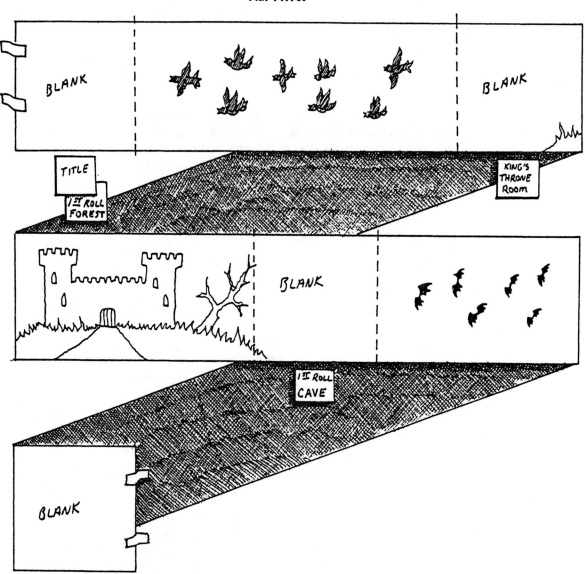

With this double rolling scenery rack, it doesn't matter which film is on top when sliding back and forth across the projection stage. As noted earlier, both rolls must be attached so that the plastic issues from underneath the rollers. This pulls the acetate down against the projection stage for good focus.

The basic construction of this frame is simply an elongation of the previous one; the finished rack is illustrated in figure 11.9.

■*Supplies:* approximately 16' of 1"-x-2" lumber, four 10½" lengths of closet pole, 2' of ½" dowel, ¾" wood screws, 1½" wood screws, 6' of 1½"-wide 1"-thick foam rubber, contact cement, electric drill, ½" drill bit, smaller bits for pilot holes, screwdriver, wood glue, 1' of 1"-x-2" board for handles, four screw-on or bolted knobs

■*Directions:* Measure the front base of the overhead projector, add approximately 28" to it, and cut two lengths of 1"-x-2" pieces that size. Measure the side base of the projector, add 2" or 3" to it, and cut two lengths of 1"-x-2" to that size. Glue and screw these pieces on edge into a frame with the shorter pieces to the outside.

Cut four 9" lengths of 1"-x-2" pieces. Center and drill a ½" hole 1½" from one end of each piece. Work the bit through these holes so that a ½" dowel will twist easily in them. Glue and screw the 1"-x-2" pieces upright in each corner with flat sides facing the length of the frame.

Cut four 1' lengths of 1"-x-2" pieces. Center and drill ½" holes in the same fashion. Glue and screw them to the inside length of the frame approximately 3" away from the 9" sections in the corners.

Center and drill ½" wide holes about 1" deep in both ends of each 10½" length of closet pole. Cut eight 3" lengths of ½" dowel. Glue one end of each dowel. Insert one in each piece of closet pole. After tapping it into place, slip it into the hole of the 1"-x-2" post. Align the other hole in the dowel with the hole in the opposite 1"-x-2" post. Insert the other glued dowel and tap it into place. Do this with all four dowels.

Cut four handles from the 1"-x-2" board. Drill a ½" hole near one end and attach knob at the other end. Glue end of protruding dowel and place handle over it. Add a setscrew to prevent twisting.

Cut three lengths of foam rubber for each closet pole, making sure they will encircle the pole completely. Apply contact cement to closet pole and attach foam rubber strips.

Triple Rolling Scenery Rack

The triple rack's top-to-bottom roll allows vertical movement for falling, climbing, and ascending or descending scenic pans. (See fig. 11.11.) Although it's usually the least-used roll on the rack, the unusual (and unexpected) scenery movement it allows makes it worthwhile.

Fig. 11.11.

Because the 1"-x-2" posts that carry this roll are closer to the projector, it's possible for them to support a staging area above the overhead projector's projection stage. This securely supports a transparency scene while rolling scenery operates underneath it. (See fig. 11.12.) For instance, the transparency of a night sky with full moon and stars can remain stationary while a rolling scene of forest moves beneath it. The combined effect is very cinematic and completely believable.

Fig. 11.12.

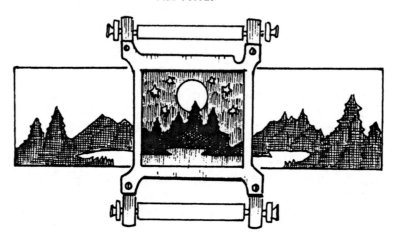

This rack stage also provides a smooth base for operating overhead projector puppets. Additional scene materials can snag these figures, causing jerky movements and (in worst-case scenarios) unintended exits into the scenery rolls.

As this level is slightly above the projection stage, absolutely clear focus isn't possible for both of them. Rather than have one go completely out of focus, adjust the control knob until the difference is split between both levels. The slight softening in focus is usually not objectionable, especially when viewed in larger rooms.

Storyboarding is vital to plan the necessary blanks between vertical visuals so that scenery from the other rolls and transparencies can be used. A vertical storyboard is similar to previous ones. (See fig. 11.13.)

It's important that this vertical roll be uppermost when sliding across the projection stage of the overhead projector so that it doesn't get caught on the edges of the side-to-side rolls.

Fig. 11.13.

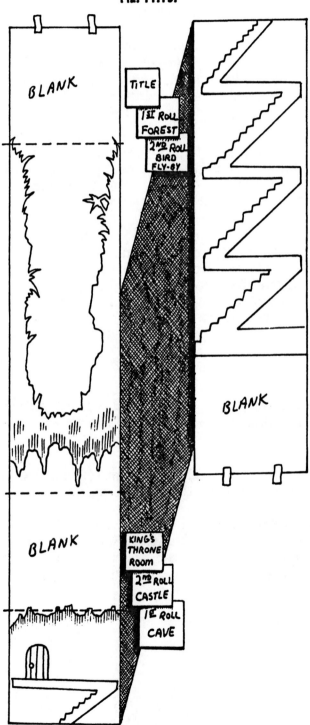

Because this more-elaborate rack (fig. 11.11) is an extension of the previous one, the materials list and directions include information regarding only the addition. The rack stage's materials and directions follow below.

■*Supplies:* 4' of 1"-x-4" lumber, two 12" lengths of closet pole, 1' of ½" dowel, four handles of 1"-x-2" lumber, four screw-on or bolted knobs, 6' of 1½" wide 1" thick foam rubber, contact cement, electric drill, ½" drill bit, smaller bits for pilot holes, screwdriver, wood glue

■*Directions:* Measure the height of the overhead projector's base. Add 1" to this measurement and cut four pieces of 1"-x-4" to this length.

Drill a ½" hole 1½" from the end of each piece and 1" from the side. Glue and screw these pieces to the front and back of the scenery rack approximately 12½" apart.

Center and drill ½"-wide holes about 1" deep in both ends of each 12" length of closet pole. Cut four 3" lengths of ½" dowel. Glue one end of each dowel. Insert one in each piece of closet pole. After tapping it into place, slip it into the hole of the 1"-x-2" post. Align the other hole in the dowel with the hole in the opposite 1"-x-2" post. Insert the other glued dowel and tap it into place.

Cut two handles from the 1"-x-4" board. Drill a ½" hole near one end and attach knob at the other end. Glue end of protruding dowel and place handle over it. Add a setscrew to prevent twisting.

Cut three lengths of foam rubber for each closet pole, making sure they will encircle the pole completely. Apply contact cement to closet pole and attach foam rubber strips.

Rack Stage

■*Supplies:* One ¼" plywood square measuring approximately 16" x 16", four 1"-long ¼" machine bolts, electric drill with ¼" bit, saber saw, 12"-x-12" sheet of acetate, strapping tape

■*Directions:* Drill a ¼"-wide hole about 1" deep in the top of each newly attached 1"-x-4" posts for the vertical scene roll on the side closest to the projector.

Measure between these holes and trim the square of ¼" plywood so that it will rest on these posts without a great deal of overlap. Then cut a square out of the plywood to match the projection stage of the overhead projector, leaving approximately a 1½" border all the way around.

Drill ¼"-wide holes through the plywood to match the ones in the posts and secure the square with 1"-long ¼" machine bolts. Cover the opening with clear acetate, trimming it to size before taping it down.

Most of these squares will require a notch in the upper right corner to accommodate the post holding the projector's reflecting lens. Again, as overhead projectors are a rather diverse lot, they will have to be shaped according to the machine available.

12

Backstage Hints

As productions become more complex and performances more formal, backstage movement and clutter increases. Here are a few helpful hints to prevent pandemonium behind the screen.

SAFETY LIGHTS

Safety was tangentially referred to in the context of lighting instruments (fig. 1.1), but the precautions are certainly worth repeating. When performing on a curtained stage, place low-wattage safety lights near traffic areas and projection tables rather than relying on light spill from overhead projectors. Cardboard or blue Roscolux shades can be attached to the lights to prevent their illumination from reaching the shadow screen.

Fluorescent tape is also available from theater supply stores for the same purpose.

STAGE LOCATIONS

If the shadow screen and projection table have to be moved to make room for other activities, mark ("spike") the stage at the corners of the screen and the legs of the table with masking tape so that the table can be replaced with minimum effort.

PUPPET AND PROP VISIBILITY

If backstage darkness causes puppets and props to blend into the color of the tabletop, cover the table with a contrasting paper prior to setting up the overhead projector. Use additional tables rather than the floor to place shadow puppets before and after performance. Larger props such as profile masks can be hung with Velcro from the side supports flanking the shadow screen.

PROJECTED SCENERY STABILITY

With all the activity at the overhead projector, it's very easy to nudge the reflecting lens or the body of the machine, causing the projection to veer off the shadow screen. Before performance, tighten any restraining nuts on the reflecting lens or use masking tape to hold them in a set position. Tape the casing of the overhead projector (or the rack it's within) to the tabletop.

PUPPETEER MOVEMENT

With longer productions, walking on your knees to operate screen shadow puppets becomes tiresome and painful. If a higher shadow screen isn't possible, the solution is a wheeled puppeteer's stool. (See fig. 12.1.) Constructed of two plywood circles, a connecting rod of galvanized steel, and caster wheels, these zippy little contraptions afford enormous ease of movement backstage. They're not expensive or difficult to make but do take some getting used to. Tipping over is common even among professional puppeteers. (At least you don't fall very far.) Also, they're great fun to play with, so make sure your students are disciplined enough to use them properly.

Fig. 12.1.

■*Supplies:* two 10"-12" circles of ¾" plywood, one 3"-7"-long piece of 1½" interior diameter galvanized steel pipe threaded at both ends, two flanges for same-diameter pipe, four heavy-duty caster wheels, saber saw, electric drill with ¼" bit, sixteen 1" long ¼" machine bolts with washers and wingnuts, eight ¾" woodscrews, 2"-3"-thick foam rubber pad, contact cement, 18"-x-18" square of fabric or vinyl, staplegun with ¼" staples

■*Directions:* Cut circles out of plywood with saber saw. Glue the foam rubber pad to one circle, cover it with material, and staple it in place. Place caster wheels toward the outer rim of the second circle; then mark and drill holes to attach them with machine bolts.

Center and screw a flange underneath the seat circle and another on top of the wheel circle. Connect the circles with threaded galvanized pipe, the height of which will vary according to the height of the puppeteer. Please note that shorter stools are more stable than taller ones.

Index

About the Authors

Donna Wisniewski graduated with a Bachelor's Degree in Graphic Design from American University. After working with some of the leading design firms in the Washington, D.C. area, she formed her own studio. Countering a slow summer with a part-time position with a local puppetry troupe, she enjoyed the profession so much that she went into it full-time, eventually becoming the company's director. Hiring her future husband David in 1975, she continued with the troupe until 1980, when the duo founded Clarion Shadow Theatre.

David Wisniewski joined Ringling Brothers and Barnum & Bailey Circus soon after high school in 1972. After touring with that show for two seasons and a stint with Circus Vargas, a California-based tent circus, he returned home to the Washington, D.C. area. After freelancing as an actor and prop designer for theater and opera companies, he was hired by Donna Harris in 1975 as a puppeteer. They were married six months later.

Besides his work in shadow puppetry, David has developed his papercutting and writing skills to produce six highly regarded children's picture books, featuring intricate multilevel papercut illustrations.

Clarion Shadow Theatre has performed for thousands of children and adults in the Washington, D.C. region, appearing at the Smithsonian Institution's Discovery Theater program and Kennedy Center's Programs for Children and Youth. The troupe has garnered two grants from the prestigious Henson Foundation (founded by the late Jim Henson, founder of The Muppets, to "foster excellence in the field of American puppetry") and a Citation of Excellence from UNIMA (Union Internationale de Marionette).

The Wisniewskis have also conducted many in-services and workshops in their unique form of shadow puppetry, working extensively with the Wolf Trap Institute for Early Learning Through the Arts over a ten-year period.

The Washington Post has hailed their work as "stunning" and "brilliant," regarding them as "the leading figures of shadow puppetry in the United States." *The Christian Science Monitor* has also profiled their work, calling them "shadow theater's cutting edge."

225

from *Teacher Ideas Press*

GLUES, BREWS, AND GOOS
Recipes and Formulas for Almost Any Classroom Project
Diana F. Marks

You've got to have it! This indispensable activity book pulls together hundreds of practical, easy recipes and formulas for classroom projects. From paints and salt map mixtures to volcanic action formulas, these kid-tested projects make learning authentic and enjoyable. All projects use ingredients that are easy to find and processes that are up-to-date. **Grades K–6.**
xvi, 179p. 8½x11 paper ISBN 1-56308-362-0

SCIENCE THROUGH CHILDREN'S LITERATURE, 2d Edition
Carol M. Butzow and John W. Butzow

The Butzows' groundbreaking, critically acclaimed, and best-selling resource has been thoroughly revised and updated with new titles and new activities for today's classroom. More than 30 exciting instructional units integrate all areas of the curriculum and serve as models to educators at all levels. Adopted as a supplementary text in schools of education nationwide, this resource features outstanding children's fiction books that are rich in scientific concepts yet equally well known for their strong story lines and universal appeal. **Grades K–3.**
xix, 205p. 8½x11 paper ISBN 1-56308-651-4

MULTICULTURAL FOLKTALES
Readers Theatre for Elementary Students
Suzanne I. Barchers

Introduce your students to other countries and cultures through these engaging readers theatre scripts based upon traditional folk and fairy tales. Representing more than 30 countries and regions, the 40 reproducible scripts are accompanied by presentation suggestions and recommendations for props and delivery. **Grades 1–5.**
xxi, 188p. 8½x11 paper ISBN 1-56308-760-X

SUPER SIMPLE STORYTELLING
A Can-Do Guide for Every Classroom, Every Day
Kendall Haven

Aside from guides to more than 40 powerful storytelling exercises, you'll find the Golden List of what an audience really needs from storytelling, a proven, step-by-step system for successfully learning and remembering a story, and the Great-Amazing-Never-Fail Safety Net to prevent storytelling disasters. This system has been successfully used by more than 15,000 educators across the country. **All Levels.**
xxvii, 229p. 8½x11 paper ISBN 1-56308-681-6

MORE SOCIAL STUDIES THROUGH CHILDREN'S LITERATURE
An Integrated Approach
Anthony D. Fredericks

These dynamic literature-based activities will help you energize the social studies curriculum and implement national and state standards. Each of these 33 units offers book summaries, social studies topic areas, critical thinking questions, and dozens of easy-to-do activities for every grade level. The author also gives practical guidelines for integrating literature across the curriculum, lists of Web sites useful in social studies classes, and annotated bibliographies of related resources. **Grades K–5.**
xix, 225p. 8½x11 paper ISBN 1-56308-761-8

For a free catalog or to place an order, please contact:
Teacher Ideas Press • Dept. B050 • P.O. Box 6633 • Englewood, CO • 80155-6633
800-237-6124 • www.lu.com/tip • Fax: 303-220-8843